HOW TO BUY A HOUSE

Kirstie Allsopp & Phil Spencer

HOW TO BUY
A HOUSE

HODDER &
STOUGHTON

First published in 2004 by Penguin Books Ltd

This edition first published in Great Britain in 2014 by Hodder & Stoughton
An Hachette UK company

1

A CIP catalogue record for this title is available from the British Library

Trade Paperback ISBN 978 1 444 79063 4
Ebook ISBN 978 1 444 79064 1

Typeset in Celeste by Palimpsest Book Production Ltd,
Falkirk, Stirlingshire

Printed and bound in Great Britain by Clays Ltd, St Ives plc

Hodder & Stoughton policy is to use papers that are natural, renewable
and recyclable products and made from wood grown in sustainable forests.
The logging and manufacturing processes are expected to conform to the
environmental regulations of the country of origin.

Hodder & Stoughton Ltd
338 Euston Road
London NW1 3BH

www.hodder.co.uk

This book is dedicated to Fiona Hindlip who was brave in all things, especially house hunting.

"So long lives this and this give life to thee."

CONTENTS

INTRODUCTION

Ten years ago, Phil and I first sat down to write this book. What we wanted to produce was a clear, easy-to-follow guide for anyone looking for a home, or indeed anyone who has found one but is unclear about what happens next.

I think we cracked it, and so did lots of you, if the kind of comments we received are anything to go by. But we know a lot more now than we did then, partly because our lives have changed so much and we have another ten years of house-hunting experience.

Between us, we now have four sons, two stepsons and two dogs. Phil and his family live between south London and Kent and we live between west London and Devon.

The last decade has also been one of change for the economy. The collapse of the subprime mortgage market in the USA created chaos, confidence in global financial institutions was eroded and seven trillion dollars was wiped off global stock markets in 2008. One of the knock-on effects of the credit crunch was a downturn in the UK property market. There was a fall in property prices and house sale transactions but, more importantly for buyers, there was a tightening of lending criteria and mortgage approvals went down. Property prices in some areas have returned to what they were pre-crash but not in other regions.

But enough of the doom and gloom, you didn't buy this book to be put off finding your dream home. Yes, you might need to jump through a few more hoops to secure a mortgage, and interest-only deals are fewer on the ground, but there is help available.

Phil and I have seen more highs and lows, more bad choices and good decisions, more sainted sellers and rogue agents and more hopeless solicitors, risk-averse surveyors and reluctant lenders than you can shake a stick at. So we thought now was the time to revisit this book: to update some bits and reiterate others, all in order to ensure you have a useful sword and shield in the great home-buying battle.

Taking the first step towards buying a home is one of the biggest financial commitments you'll ever make, but it is also one of the most exciting things you'll ever do. Some people only buy one property in their entire lives and very few are involved in more than four property transactions, yet most folk head out into the world of estate agents, mortgage advisers, surveyors and removal men completely unaided. Would you head out to sea with no compass, radio or flares? No – not unless you were crazy. Yet that is exactly what happens when people attempt to buy houses. So that is why we are here, to give you the information you need to cross those treacherous seas and find the home of your dreams.

> ## We have been involved in literally hundreds of property purchases and have come across every possible scenario.

Between us we have personally purchased nine properties, and as professional homes search consultants we have guided people through property purchases for many years. As a result we have been involved in literally hundreds of deals and have come across every possible scenario. There is little in this game that surprises us and less that shocks us. And we love it – we love the houses and flats, the A to Z, the leases, the surveyors' reports, the deal making and we love the agents! We want you, too, to benefit from our knowledge, so that your house-hunt is as successful as possible.

To do this you must ensure that you stand head and shoulders above other buyers. Therefore, our biggest trade secret is this: be very, very nice to estate agents. Until you can learn to love, or at the very least like, estate agents all our other advice is, at best, only 50 per cent effective.

We realize this is a revolutionary concept but, like all the best ideas, it's simple and it works. This approach has served us very well. If you're nice to them and build up a good working relationship they won't want to see you walk away with a dud house. Granted, it takes practice, and there are some agents who would try the patience of a saint, but they are rarer than you think. Most agents are just trying to keep body and soul together and pay their own mortgage; it's not their fault that the product they are selling plays a uniquely important part in your life.

When you tell your friends and colleagues that you are trying to buy a house or flat you will be inundated with horror stories; stick your fingers in your ears and walk away. Home buying isn't all bad. It's like having a baby; some people have good experiences, some bad, but once you've got your new baby all the pain is forgotten. This book is your pain relief. Some people don't need it, but it's nice to know that you've got the option. Focus on the job in hand, don't skip the boring bits and push when we tell you to.

1

MONEY, MONEY, MONEY

If you haven't already binned this book because we've lectured you about being nice to agents then perhaps we're in this together for the long haul.

Before you do anything else you must find out what you can afford to spend. Never, ever go out searching for a house until you have arranged your financing. There is no quicker route to disappointment than to view properties which you then discover you can't afford, and you will be wasting both your own and the estate agents' time.

Start by getting an idea of what you can borrow as a mortgage. In the past, lenders simply multiplied your income to calculate how much to lend, usually up to 3.5 times your single salary or 2.5 times for a joint salary. Now, the key for lenders is affordability – what you can realistically afford to spend on your monthly repayments. They look at your income compared to your outgoings, so you will need to work out your home budget – this should take into account your regular monthly outgoings, direct debits, credit card charges and loan repayments, all bills including mobile phone, internet, electricity, gas, food, etc. Having completed this you can approach your bank or mortgage broker knowing what you can realistically afford in monthly repayments.

The days of the 100 per cent mortgage are behind us. You will need a cash deposit of at least 5 per cent of the purchase price, yet to get a good rate of interest on your loan you will often need a deposit of over 20 per cent of the home value. A good rule of thumb is the bigger the deposit, the better the rate and the lower your monthly repayments will be.

Once you have calculated how much you can borrow and added on any capital you will realize from the sale of your existing property (but be sensible about the amount you're likely to achieve), you need to minus the related costs of moving and purchasing: agent's fee, removal expenses, stamp duty, solicitor's and surveyor's fees. And, voilà, this should give you a figure which indicates how much you can afford to spend on a property.

Never, ever go out searching for a house until you have arranged your financing.

KIRSTIE'S TOP TIP

Banks are looking to loan money to fiscally responsible people. Lending criteria are much tougher these days and affordability and credit checks will determine to a large extent whether you get your mortgage or not.

- The banks will want to see your accounts for the last three years to make sure you are a safe bet financially. If you have bought this book because you are looking to buy a home in the future, my advice would be to get you finances in order as soon as possible.

- There are certain red flags that lenders look for to indicate whether you are responsible with your money or not.

- Make sure you set up a direct debit so you pay at least the minimum repayment on credit cards and don't miss a month.

- Don't withdraw cash on your credit card, it is much more expensive than withdrawing money from you current account and suggests you are desperate.

- Avoid payday loans at any cost. Not only are the interest rates crippling but some mortgage lenders see payday loans as a sign that you can't manage your money.

WHAT WILL IT COST?

Average costs for a purchase of £175,000

Legal fees	(£750 + 20% VAT) =	£900.00
Survey	(£500 + 20% VAT) =	£600.00
Mortgage arrangement fee	=	£500.00
Searches	=	£300.00
Stamp duty	=	£1,750.00
TOTAL CASH	**= £4,050.00**

MOVING COSTS

Don't forget to include these additional costs of moving, if relevant, in your calculations.

- Removal van

- Reconnection charges for electricity and gas

- Installation of telephone and internet

- Plumbing-in costs for white goods

- Redirection of post

- Change of address notification

- Essential decorative or building works

THE BASICS

This summarizes your position as a buyer and you need to ensure your estate agent has this information. Use this as a starting point to compile your house-hunting business cards (see our examples on page 44).

- total spend (mortgage + capital – moving costs)

- ability to move (cash/mortgage buyer, chain?)

- location required

- type of property

- willing to extend or refurbish?

- size of property

- your name and current address

- solicitor's details

MORTGAGES – SIGNING YOUR LIFE AWAY . . .

Once you have an idea of how much you will be able to borrow and what you can afford in monthly repayments, it's time to consider the kind of mortgage you want. The variety of mortgages available is bewildering: there are over two hundred lenders offering thousands of products.

For most of us, getting a mortgage will be one of the biggest financial decisions we make in our lifetime and you will spend a large part of your life paying off your mortgage, so it is crucial to understand as much as you can about them. The internet is the obvious place to do some research; there are numerous mortgage guides, which will walk you through the process and offer good tips on what to look out for so you can feel confident that you are in a position to make the right decision.

> **PHIL'S TOP TIP**
>
> **While the internet is a valuable tool for getting information it does also have its drawbacks. Mortgage comparison websites will offer you thousands of deals in an instant, but the downside is that most comparison websites do not provide advice, so think twice before you click the 'apply' button.**

So where do you start? Begin with your bank: go to their website and see what they can offer you. Then you have a point of comparison and you can judge other mortgages accordingly. Try www.yourmortgage.co.uk. This is the website of the consumer magazine *Your Mortgage* and has up-to-date information on the best deals and worst rip-offs. Also check out The Money Advice Service, www.moneyadviceservice.org, this is an independent service set up by the government that offers impartial advice on money matters, including mortgages. Each type of mortgage has its advantages and disadvantages, but direct comparisons can be hard to make because deals vary so much.

THE INTERNET AND HOME BUYING

When Phil and I started finding houses for clients the internet was still in its infancy and many people were still offline. This was before tablets, smartphones and internet banking, a time when many solicitors relied solely on the fax machine and postal service; now you can even do your own conveyancing online. However, this is more risky and we would advise you to hire a professional, either a solicitor or a licensed conveyancer. But it is definitely worthwhile double-checking that your solicitor uses email, and can send a text. If you spend the majority of your time on your smartphone and computer and much of your communication is via the web it would drive you crazy if your solicitor thought a tablet was a type of Scottish toffee!

KIRSTIE SAYS

"The internet is an invaluable research tool at this stage. You can learn about mortgages, compare deals, find a good local solicitor all from the comfort of your own home. Internet property search engines have also come on leaps and bounds since we first wrote this book. Now 90 per cent of people start their search online and most major property search websites have apps you can download with interactive maps, text and email

alerts, area guides and house price data. However, later on when you begin searching, there is no substitute for going out to meet the estate agents, building up good relationships and staying in touch by telephone. Most agents will call their favourite buyers to tell them about new instructions long before they are posted on the agency's website. Although nearly all estate agents have websites, some of which are excellent, you may find that when you ring up to make an appointment to view something you spotted while surfing the net at 2 a.m., it's gone – good stuff goes fast in any market."

Mortgage payments usually account for 15–25 per cent of people's income, but it all depends on the size of your deposit, how long you borrow the money for and how much you spend on other things. As long as you've saved up a deposit and budgeted for all the extra expenses when you move, you'll only need to work out your existing monthly outgoings and deduct this figure from your after-tax income to be left with a good idea of how much you can afford as a monthly payment.

As we discussed in the introduction, the global financial crash of 2008 had a huge impact on our economy and subsequently the UK property market. The credit crunch did exactly what it said on the tin: it squeezed the available credit, lending criteria were tightened considerably, and we are still feeling the effects today. However, there is cause to be optimistic: the economy is moving in the right direction, unemployment is down and mortgage approvals are up.

Although there are a myriad mortgage deals on the market with alternatives within each of them, there are just two types of mortgage – repayment or interest-only – and the majority of mortgages agreed will be the former. Prior to 2009 it was relatively easy to agree an interest-only mortgage or to pay interest-only while you had the extra costs of setting up house, furnishing, decorating and so forth, and then swapping to a repayment option after a little while. Now, there are only a few lenders who offer this. Some banks have 'low start' deals, whereby your mortgage begins on an interest-only basis for a fixed period (usually three years) then you switch to a repayment mortgage. This seems like a sensible plan to us. Although neither of us is a qualified mortgage adviser what we *can* do is explain the jargon and some of the advantages and disadvantages of the options.

INTEREST-ONLY MORTGAGES

With an interest-only mortgage you pay only the interest on the loan each month. So if, for example, you borrow £100,000 interest-only and make the minimum monthly payments, you still owe £100,000 at the end of the mortgage term. This means you need to find the money to cover your debt, so you also need to contribute towards a stock market investment plan like an ISA (individual savings account), a pension or an endowment. The advantage is that these 'methods' can be tax efficient and if the growth rate of the investment exceeds expectations, you could be left with an additional lump sum at the end.

Interest-only lending accounted for a third of mortgages agreed in 2007. They were hugely popular with first-time buyers and young people who didn't have large deposits and wanted to escape high rents, particularly in inner cities. However, a large proportion of these borrowers did not have repayment plans in place and the banks were accused of irresponsible lending. This has led to a tightening of lending criteria and if you apply for an interest-only mortgage now you will have to prove you have a robust plan in place to repay the loan at the end of the mortgage term and not just rely on property prices rising to repay the loan.

It is important to remember that even if you have a solid repayment vehicle in place *the value of your investment can go down as well as up,* and so there are no guarantees. Many of them, particularly endowments, have performed very badly recently.

REPAYMENT MORTGAGES

With a repayment loan your monthly payments are higher as they contribute towards paying off the total amount borrowed as well as the interest on the debt. There is a specified repayment period and the mortgage is guaranteed to be repaid in full at the end of the term. Very little of the amount borrowed is paid off in the early years of the mortgage (the amount paid off increases each year) so if you move again in the short term it's likely you'll need to take out a new twenty- to twenty-five-year mortgage. On the flip side, it removes the risk of having an investment which is dependent on the stock market, and you're less likely to suffer from negative equity because your debt will be reducing month by month. If you have a repayment mortgage you should also take out a mortgage protection policy to ensure your loan is paid off if you die (unless you have cover arranged elsewhere).

KIRSTIE SAYS

"This is complicated stuff, and not everyone finds figures easy to grasp. I can remember the exact layout of a house I viewed for five minutes five years ago, but when faced with a spreadsheet I want to weep. If you suffer from number blindness, don't be afraid to ask! Make it very clear that you don't understand, and don't stay quiet for fear that the mortgage provider won't want to lend money to someone who can't calculate interest. We all have different talents – after all, your financial adviser probably has no idea of how to do your job."

KIRSTIE SAYS

"When we first published this book in 2004 the following was true: do not think of your mortgage in terms of a loan, that suggests an act of generosity – you are buying the money from the mortgage company and, what's more, they want to sell it to you. Interestingly, this is

not the case any more. In 2006 you were pretty much guaranteed a mortgage but lenders were burnt when the bottom fell out of the subprime mortgage market in the USA and, as a result, they are now much more cautious."

INTEREST-RATE OPTIONS

Once you've decided whether you are going to make payments on the capital or not then you can turn your mind to interest-rate options.

Competition among banks and building societies means there's a multitude of different ways to calculate interest. Here again, there are two main choices – a variable rate or a fixed rate. Just to confuse things, there are also ways of combining these options so part of your loan is fixed and the rest variable.

Variable rate

This is the simplest form of loan. Lenders' standard variable rates are based on the Bank of England's base rate and generally move up and down with changes in base rate. There are usually no early redemption penalties on these mortgages, but the unpredictability of interest rates makes it hard to budget accurately.

Fixed rate

Your monthly payment is fixed for a specified period (typically two to five years) irrespective of changes to the Bank of England's base rate or your lender's standard variable rate. Interest rates move in both directions, so remember that while sometimes you can benefit, you may also be trapped in what becomes an uncompetitive rate. It's easy to budget and possible to benefit from lower rates in the first few years, but redemption penalties will usually apply if you change your mortgage during the penalty period.

Discount rate

A discount mortgage offers a reduction on the lender's variable rate for a set period. As the lender's standard rate moves up and down, so the discounted rate moves by the same amount. Be aware that there is normally a redemption penalty if you change mortgage, and at the end of the discounted period your payments will increase as the mortgage reverts to the lender's standard variable rate.

Tracker

Tracker mortgages follow alterations to the Bank of England's base rate as soon as they occur. A lender's standard variable rate will be around 1.5 per cent above base rate, but will not *automatically* move with the base. Trackers have a smaller difference above base (say around 0.75 per cent) but are guaranteed to rise and fall with the base rate.

Capped rate

These ensure that your interest rate will not rise above a certain point (usually the standard variable rate) during the cap period. You can still benefit from a fall in rates whilst removing the danger of them rising beyond a known figure. As payback for the security of the cap, rates are higher and the cap term seldom lasts more than two or three years.

PHIL SAYS

"There's no such thing as a free lunch. If you take out a mortgage and the lender immediately gives you some cash, there'll be a cost hidden somewhere in the deal. Make sure you find out what it is. Some lenders will offer to pay the stamp duty on properties up to £250,000 (which would be £2,500) but the deal will have a higher rate of interest, so this is not free cash, rather you will simply be spreading the cost over the period of your mortgage."

Cash back

These schemes are used in conjunction with other mortgage products and are designed to pay out a lump sum when you take out your mortgage. The money can then be used for expenses such as furnishings, paying off debts and solicitor's fees.

FLEXIBLE RATE OR CURRENT ACCOUNT MORTGAGES

Flexible rate mortgages allow you to control how much you pay each month. You can overpay or underpay depending upon how flush you are at the time. Lenders impose different restrictions on the level of flexibility and you need to be well-disciplined to manage these loans. Our advice is to overpay when you can and underpay only when you really need to. Current account mortgages allow you to put all your money in one place – from your mortgage and loans to your savings and current account. Interest is calculated daily which means any cash sitting in your current account reduces your mortgage debt. If you have a mortgage of £75,000 and a current account balance of £1500 your mortgage interest will be based on the outstanding debt of £73,500.

MORTGAGE REPAYMENT VEHICLES

If you opt for an interest-only mortgage you will need a method to repay your mortgage; these are usually termed repayment vehicles.

Endowment

You contribute to an insurance company to fund an endowment savings plan. The policy is designed to make enough money to pay off the capital at the end of your mortgage term. However everything depends on the performance of the fund and many people have recently been left with a shortfall.

Pension

These work in the same way, but, as there are tax incentives, making contributions to a pension can be more tax-efficient. But using your tax-free lump sum as a mortgage repayment vehicle runs the risk of leaving you short of cash in retirement. As with endowment policies (above) they're dependent on good decisions by fund managers at the pension company.

ISA

ISA mortgages use stock-market-based investments for tax-free growth. You'll be left with a nice nest egg at the end, but as the current tax-deductible maximum contribution is £11,520 per annum it may not be enough to repay a large mortgage. You'll also need life assurance.

HIGH-RISK BORROWERS

If you're self-employed and don't have three years of accounts, do freelance work or have a poor credit rating, you'll be deemed high risk. It's still possible to borrow money, but you need to find a specialist lender. The draw-back is that the interest rate will be higher than usual, and it is also unlikely the lender will offer any deals or discounts on it. But don't let this put you off – there is a mortgage out there for everybody.

PHIL'S TOP TIP

Choose a mortgage that helps you achieve your aims. It's not just a matter of finding the lowest rate – look beyond the headlines or inducements.

PHIL'S TOP TIPS

- **Ensure you check that you'll still be able to afford the loan when any fixed rate or discounted period is over and the interest rate on your loan rises.**

- **If you go for something with an early redemption penalty it could be costly to change your lender. If you are considering this, request a calculation from your lender as to the redemption cost so you can make a decision about whether it would be worth-while to pay the penalty in order to gain the benefit of another lender's rates.**

FIRST-TIME BUYERS

Although our tactics may be miraculously helpful in finding and securing your dream home we have yet to come up with a method for growing money on trees. While ever-increasing property prices may benefit those already in the market, they are making it particularly difficult for first-time buyers (FTBs) to get a foothold on the property ladder.

But it is important to realize that it is not simply the price of property that is making life hard for FTBs; there have been a number of trends in society which have had a major impact on the property market. Thirty years ago many people left school at sixteen and started work, but remained living at home. They then, perhaps, got engaged in their very early twenties, but continued to live at home until they had enough money saved up to put down a deposit on a house, get married and move in together. Nowadays things are very different. Many more people go to college or university; the average age when people marry has shot up, as has the average age when they have their first child; and far fewer people remain living at home once they have begun working. This means that instead of coming to the market as a couple in their early twenties, with five or six years' worth of combined savings to put down as a deposit, the majority of people start in their late twenties, single and already burdened with debts.

MODERN MARRIAGES

Opinion is always divided as to whether the market will go up or down, but it is unlikely things will get any easier for FTBs. As a result many people are creating modern marriages: partnerships with friends, colleagues or siblings which allow them to get that longed-for foothold. A modern marriage is an excellent method of buying property and the last thing we want is to be discouraging, so please regard the following as things to think about, not words of warning.

The majority of people who move in together are 'in love', but if this is not the case you have to think very carefully about how you are going to cope with living with another person and perhaps their partners. Modern marriages can get crowded – just because you are both single when you buy doesn't mean it will stay that way.

All the information, tips and recipes in this book are doubly important if you are buying together and, even if you are a couple, the same advice still applies. It also helps to establish some ground rules right from the beginning, especially as regards finance. All the buying costs must be split fifty/fifty. It is most straightforward if you share equally all the costs. But if one of you is contributing more capital than the other you should agree, when buying, how the increase, or decrease, should be divided. One way of doing this is described in the example that follows.

JANE AND SARAH HAVE A TOTAL BUDGET OF £160,000

Jane has £9,400 in savings and her parents will contribute £12,000.

Sarah has a £15,000 legacy from her father and £2,000 in savings.

They buy a house for £152,000, having taken out a mortgage for £121,600 with a deposit of £30,400. They put the remaining £8,000 in a joint account. The stamp duty, legal fees, etc. come to £3,875 and they spend the remaining £4,125 on painting the kitchen cabinets, putting in a new worktop, redecorating the sitting room and buying a sofa.

After four years the house sells for £179,000. How do they calculate what they take away? First they look at what they each put in. They paid the mortgage equally.

	Jane	Sarah
Initial contribution:	21,400	17,000
Mortgage payments:	11,675	11,675
Total:	33,075	28,675

Combined total: £61,750

From the £179,000 they received for the house they deduct:

Outstanding mortgage:	£98,250
Estate agent's fees:	£3500
Legal fees:	£800

Total: £102,550

They actually receive £179,000 − £102,550 = £76,450, which they divide in proportion to what they contributed. So Jane receives £40,900.75 and Sarah, £35,549.25.

Although Jane and Sarah wouldn't be able to retire on

the profits from the sale of their house, they have come away with a nice lump of capital and have lived effectively rent-free for 4 years.

2

WHAT DO YOU WANT?

> **PHIL'S TOP TIP**
>
> **It helps to walk around an area that you are thinking of moving to and jotting down the names of the streets you like and noting those that you really aren't keen on.**

Once you've got to grips with how much you can spend on your dream home, you need to decide where you want it to be – the all-important location – and what type of property you require. Do you long for a Victorian terrace or a loft-style conversion?

LOCATION, LOCATION, LOCATION

Many of you may already have a good idea of where you want to live, but, if not, you'll be wanting advice on where to buy. Virtually every day we are asked, 'Which area is the best investment?', 'What's the new up-and-coming area?' or 'Is now a good time to buy in such and such a place?' These are the most difficult questions to answer because there are so many factors which have to be taken into account.

A common dilemma, particularly amongst first-time buyers, is that you know where you want to live, but you also know that you haven't got a snowball's chance in hell of being able to afford anything bigger than a shoe box in that location. If this is the case for you, get a map out and examine the areas on the outskirts of your preferred location – you are not the only 'refugee' who cannot afford to live where you want. Every good area creates a ripple effect: its boundaries spread, and then nearby areas are adopted.

As for the much-desired 'up-and-coming' areas, walk down any street and you can easily see whether it is coming up in the world. Are there skips or scaffolding? Any clear signs of houses being refurbished or renovated? There is much talk of the 'Starbucks effect' (i.e. watching the alteration in local businesses, seeing delicatessens or chic boutiques open up in the neighbourhood), but shops follow customers, and once the shops have changed the area has already moved 'up' and you've missed the opportunity to get in early.

People will always tell you that this or that area is your best bet, but do your own research: hit the streets, day and night, see if you like the look of an area, and of course talk to the agents. And, finally, ask yourself the 'This Life' questions on pages 38–9.

SEEK AND YE SHALL FIND

We've recommended you think about the style of the house you'd like to live in, but beware: make sure that you're not looking for a banana in a hardware store. If you want a particular type of house or flat, ensure before you start looking that it exists in your key locations. If you look and look and can't find what you want, it may be an architectural issue; the style of property you're after might never have been built in that location. Here's an opportunity to use the knowledge of local estate agents. They'll soon tell you what type of architecture dominates the locations you've stipulated. Every design has its good and bad points, and a good surveyor will know to look out for certain problems in houses or flats of a specific era.

If you are hoping to buy a flat, it will either be 'share of freehold' or 'leasehold'. We explain what these terms mean on pages 94–5, but we want to be very clear on a couple of points from the very beginning. Firstly, do not be afraid of leasehold properties. There is nothing to be scared of and, in certain areas, excluding them could reduce the number of flats available to you by 90 per cent. Secondly, it is *not* always the case that share of freehold is better than leasehold. We would rather buy a well-managed leasehold property than a share of a freehold flat in a building where no one realizes the importance of property maintenance.

THE GOOD BOOK – STYLES OF HOUSING

In the UK we are blessed with a staggeringly varied and long architectural history that is the envy of the world. Any style list that we compile would never be able to do it justice. Our bible, a book we turn to almost daily, is *The Elements of Style – An Encyclopaedia of Domestic Architectural Detail*, edited by Stephen Calloway and published by Mitchell Beazley. For anyone with more than a passing interest in architecture and design it is an absolute joy. If you are thinking of developing or refurbishing a house of any date from King Canute to 2020 it is an invaluable tool. There is also a fantastic new mobile and tablet app called Pevsner's Architectural Glossary. With it you can walk through over 134 historic buildings, and the glossary of architectural terms will soon have you knowing your Gothic arch from your Ogee arch.

KIRSTIE SAYS

"My dream house is a seventeenth-century stone-built farmhouse. This type of house is unlikely to have much in the way of internal decoration, i.e. cornicing or ceiling roses, and it may well be uneconomical to heat, although there's probably a fireplace in virtually every room. The windows rattle, the kitchen is bound to be at the back of the house in a dark little corner and the house will have been built for practicality rather than beauty. But if it's managed to stay standing for four hundred years,

it'll probably stick around for another four hundred, however terrible the survey is."

Early Housing

Houses built roughly in the period 1350–1800 are described as British vernacular; in a time before trucks or trains the building materials available locally dictated how houses were built. For example, you won't find a thatched house three hundred miles from the nearest reed beds or a pale yellow Cotswold stone house in Dundee. Regional differences weren't only determined by the availability of local materials but also by the area's wealth and the ability of the local people to retain some of that wealth. For example, social and political circumstances favoured the farmers of Kent and they were celebrated for their wealth long before the end of the Middle Ages. Thousands of timber-framed houses still survive, yet in poorer areas, where the farmers were unable to afford the luxury of permanent homes, houses fell into ruins after only a generation or so. The long-established concentration of wealth in the south and east of England led to the early development of vernacular housing there.

The type of vernacular architecture everyone considers at some stage in their lives is the thatched cottage, but, take note, they often have low ceilings, the windows can be small, making the rooms quite dark, and, like many older houses, there is a strong possibility the building is listed. This means that any alterations you wish to make to the house will be severely restricted. So, be wary, if you are six foot three, give up on the idea of living in a three-hundred-year-old thatched cottage.

Georgian

The vast majority of us when asked our favourite type of architecture say Georgian. Yet often we're unaware that this period stretches over a hundred years, from George I to George IV, and, unless you are a student of architecture, you are likely to lump the Queen Anne style (1702–14) and the Regency period (1812–20) into this era as well.

It is the pleasing symmetry and high-ceilinged rooms of the Georgian style that appeal to us so much. Developments in glass production meant that window panes could be larger, hence the lighter rooms. The 'doll's house' look with sash windows is most typical of the Georgian style. Many of our towns and cities including Bath, London and Edinburgh are dominated by Georgian architecture.

Victorian

After the Georges came Queen Victoria (1837–1901) and her son Edward VII (1901–10). Victorian and Edwardian architecture comprises a huge proportion of what is available to buy in today's market. One of the foremost characteristics of the Victorian house is the bay window; it allowed more light into the front room and gave a good view of the comings and goings of neighbours. The decoration of ceilings became increasingly elaborate and even the most modest houses had moulded cornices and central ceiling roses. The other essential feature of the Victorian house is the fireplace. This consisted of two parts: the manufactured cast-iron grate and the chimney piece made from marble, slate or wood, depending on the means of the owner.

Edwardian

Victorian values and style did not come to a halt with the Queen's death in 1901, but continued into the Edwardian era, with only subtle variations until the watershed of World War I. One innovation of the Edwardian period was the mansion block, perhaps precipitated by the invention of the electric lift or 'ascending carriage'. Improvements to plumbing and drainage also made a big difference: flats could now have central heating and a twenty-four-hour supply of hot water, and be hygienically linked to the sewerage system.

Within both the Victorian and Edwardian eras there were those who fought against the prevailing trend. Among these were the followers of the Arts and Crafts Movement (1860–1925) and Art Nouveau (1888–1905). These movements rejected increasing industrialization and pleaded for honesty in materials and craftsmanship. Ironically, many of the design elements – the red brick, white woodwork and features such as porches and oriel windows – were adopted by commercial developers and used in the 1920s.

1920s and 30s

This period was dominated by the Art Deco style, named after the Paris exhibition of 1925, the Exposition Internationale des Arts Décoratifs et Industriels Modernes. The most common characteristics of the style are metal windows, sometimes rounded in the 'suntrap' style, and the use of the sunburst or sunray pattern in doors and windows; there were also revivalist trends including 'Tudorbethan' or 'Stockbroker Tudor'. Houses built in this style are black and white, half-timbered with gabled, leaded windows and are particularly prominent in the suburbs.

Post-war

The war years had a dramatic affect on house building – there was neither money nor manpower to build properties. But in the years immediately after the war, in the rush to house returning troops, many buildings were constructed – often using designs from the pre-war period, which is why there is a noticeable similarity between 30s and 50s architecture. As prosperity returned, building continued in earnest and stark new styles emerged, including the advent of the 60s tower block.

Developments in the production and use of concrete resulted in new designs and some interesting experiments. Little changed in domestic architecture though – families still required bedrooms, bathrooms and reception rooms.

Contemporary

Today there is the opportunity to buy or commission an extraordinary variety of contemporary properties, and the majority of buyers consider new build to be best. But new-build properties are getting smaller – the average size has reduced by 30 per cent in the last 30 years. Decent family space is increasingly hard to come by in newer homes, so you may be better off looking at more established developments from the 80s and 90s. When you are looking at new build make sure you shop around. There is a vast difference in standards and it is not always cost related. Do *not* allow yourself to be seduced by the show home. Developers pick the best and biggest property on a plot and deck it out with plasma screens and snazzy bathrooms to sell you a grand lifestyle.

ANOTHER TACK – AUCTIONS

When we were home search agents there was nothing that made our hearts sink more than clients coming to us in search of the unusual. Despite what we are led to believe by glossy magazines, the countryside is not awash with disused public buildings, ripe for conversion into divine open-plan spaces. The reason for this is very simple – for every ten, twenty or even fifty village houses there are only one or at most two chapels, schools or pubs, which for the most part are still being used for their intended purpose. By looking for this type of project you are reducing by 90 per cent the number of properties available to you. But you've bought our book, so we will help all we can. If you wish to do the conversion yourself, you are most likely to find what you are looking for at auction. Many purchasers find the idea of buying a home at auction terrifying; maybe it's because they feel there is something so definite and inescapable about the moment the auctioneer's gavel comes down, and buyers fear being caught up in the competitive atmosphere of the auction room and paying far more than they intended for their new house.

The joy of an auction purchase is that you can look the opposition, i.e. the other potential purchasers, in the eye and there is no gazumping. The key to a successful auction purchase is to arm yourself with as much information as possible before heading into the fray. You must have a survey done (nothing new there), appoint a solicitor to obtain and check the title deeds and carry out local searches. You must also check for any special conditions of sale. It is also vital that you must have the funds available to pay the deposit (usually 10–20 per cent, as with a conventional sale) on the day of the auction. And you need to be absolutely certain that you'll be able to access funds for completion within twenty-eight days.

It is very important to familiarize yourself with the auction process. Go to a few sales simply in order to get a feel for it, and on the big day itself for God's sake leave yourself enough time to get to the sale room.

The only real downside of auction purchasing is that

the auction date, which, as we've already mentioned is effectively your exchange date, is set in stone; it cannot be changed (although it is sometimes possible to buy an auction property prior to the sale date – look out for the words 'unless previously sold' in the auction catalogue). Therefore it is only really possible to buy at auction if you have already sold your existing property. The chain, which dominates so many domestic property transactions, cannot coexist with the auction process, so you may have to spend some time in rented accommodation. This is especially the case if you are looking for a major redevelopment project as it is very possible that, however you buy the property, it will not be in a habitable condition at first.

KIRSTIE SAYS

"As the child of an auctioneer, I was literally brought up in the sale room and would not deny for a second that getting carried away with the excitement of bidding is a risk; it is the job of a good auctioneer, as it is of a good estate agent, to get the best possible price for his vendor. But remember that acceptance of your winning bid is really no different from the moment of exchange; both are the point at which you must hand over your deposit and commit yourself to buying the property."

KIRSTIE SAYS

"If you are after a project and you want to put your own stamp on a property visit www.unmodernised.com,

an un-modernized-only property database. From development plots in Manchester to derelict Georgian gems in London, this website is any wannabe developer's dream."

PHIL SAYS

"It's very easy to get carried away at auctions. It's imperative that you set yourself a top limit beforehand and stick to it. You should also try to get a seat near the back so you can see what's going on."

GOING DOOR TO DOOR

Although we constantly warn of the dangers of being too restrictive in your criteria there are times when only one house will do, or hopefully, if only for your sake, one street. Perhaps you have always longed to live in a particular road or village. Or it may be that you have loved and lost a house and you are trying to replicate it. Never a good idea, but, if you are really determined to follow your heart, we can't desert you in your hour of need.

If this *is* the case, you won't rest until you are entirely sure that no house or flat in your perfect location is about to come on the market. You'll never forgive yourself if the day you complete on another property, the perfect thing pops up. The best way to get 'closure' is to carry out a leaflet drop. Here's the recipe.

- Keep it short and sweet – so much rubbish comes through the letterbox that a great deal of mail goes directly from the doormat to the dustbin. You want to ensure that your note is read before it gets there.

- Don't mention money.

- Don't put it in an envelope, unless you know the name of the householder – many people don't open letters addressed to 'The Householder' or 'The Owner'.

- Print out your note. It's worth using good quality paper – anything that makes it stand out from the usual flyers that arrive on the mat. Then cut it into strips (you should be able to fit three notes on to a sheet of A4).

We very much want to live in Little Bedwyn, but although the local agents have been very helpful there's nothing currently available. If you are thinking of moving in the foreseeable future, please give us a ring on 07764 321 468.
Fingers crossed,
Paul and Claire Stewart

Once you've assembled a decent pile of leaflets head off to your target area. Dress tidily and try to go at the weekend – that way there is a greater chance of people being at home, and therefore a higher likelihood of making friends and gaining local knowledge. Don't ring the doorbell, just pop your leaflet through the letterbox. Inevitably you'll bump into residents of the area and you'll be amazed at the information you can glean from a chat over the garden fence – the grapevine is a wonderful thing.

If you do get a call, then, after some touching exclamations of amazement and pleasure that anyone has responded to your note, ask the vendor whether they have had a recent valuation. You don't want to get your hopes up over a house that's way beyond your budget. If the vendor has a price, make an appointment to view the property and see if you think it's reasonable. If you think the price is unrealistic, or there has been no recent valuation, you must tread very carefully.

This is the tricky bit – you need to get a fair idea of what the house is worth, but you don't want to tip off the agents that this house is for sale. So, although the vendor could get an initial valuation from a local agent, the best way to avoid the world and his wife knowing about this property is to have the valuation carried out by an agent you know and like, and who can be trusted to keep his lips zipped. But be aware that the vendor is, rather naturally, likely to be suspicious of an agent that you are too cosy with. A degree of honesty is probably best here. Explain to the vendor that you intend to pay nothing less than the going rate for his house, but that you are aware that any agent, conscious of the difference between a valuation charge (which is all he'll get if you buy the property) and his normal 2 per cent commission (which is what he'll get if he markets the property), is going to want to persuade the vendor to let him advertise the property, which is not your desired outcome. Suggest to the vendor that using your agent is almost certainly the best option. An agent's valuation is usually free, because he is hoping to receive an instruction to market the property, but in a case like this it is vital that you don't allow the vendor to attempt to mislead the agent of the circumstances to get a free valuation. Make it very clear to all involved that you are happy to pay any valuation fee.

KIRSTIE SAYS

"A great way to get an initial idea of how much a property is worth is to go online – there are numerous websites that will give you house valuation data. I like www.mouseprice.com. Type in the postcode and it will tell you when the property was last sold and for how much. You can also find out the sale price of comparable houses in the street or neighbourhood. But remember this is an inexact science – you don't know, for instance, if the house has subsequently been added to or modernized or what the interior condition is. Use house price data websites as a starting point, not as gospel."

It's a bit of a minefield, but don't panic. Instead, focus on building a trusting and understanding relationship with the vendor – if you are involved in a private sale it's the only way to proceed. If this really is the home for you, you'll find a way through; we know a number of people who have successfully found their dream home via leafleting.

THIS LIFE

You've now considered price, location and style of property, but before you rush off to start making offers here are a few other questions worth thinking about.

Ask yourself how long you imagine living in this property. We know this question may seem the 'How long is a piece of string?' type, but consider:

- Might you be going abroad for your work and renting out this home?

- How long do you imagine staying in your current job and having the same transport needs?

- How do you currently get to work and what could the alternatives be?

- Are you going to be renting out a room to help with the mortgage?

- It may sound frivolous but, if you're unsure of location, is there an area where the majority of your friends live?

- Might you think of starting a family in this home?

- If you already have a family, have you read the Ofsted reports for local schools and checked the catchment areas? Find out from the local authority the exact boundaries of these areas.

It is incredibly important to look ahead when you are buying a home. OK, so you might not have a crystal ball and be able to predict exactly what life is going to throw at you, but it pays to be prepared. If house prices fall and your property goes into negative equity, it is only a problem if you are forced to put it on the market. If your house has flexibility, then you are less likely to need to sell it. If your family grows but your house can't, then you will need to sell and possibly lose money. Buy a property with potential to extend and when your aged parents come to live with you, you won't need to move to a larger house, you can just convert the loft into a granny suite.

Similarly, if you and your partner are buying a property and you suspect for even a minute that children might be an option at some point, it is worth thinking ahead and asking yourself questions like, 'Are there good schools nearby?', 'Would this property be suitable for children?', 'Is a loft apartment on the fourth floor with no lift and a spiral staircase going to work if I find myself pregnant?'

KIRSTIE SAYS

"I had a beloved border terrier called Foxy. Ten days before I got her I completed on a one-bed, second-floor flat with no outside space. Clever, huh? You see, a lot of our advice stems from hard-learned lessons. Of course, I fell in love with Foxy and was determined that she should have a garden, so I remained at home with my parents for another year. Poor Foxy was permanently scarred – she was so bullied by my mother's cats that

she is probably the only terrier in the world who is scared of cats. But I developed the little one-bed flat, sold it at a modest profit and moved further from the shops and the station in order to afford a flat with a garden."

THE LEGAL BIT

The majority of us require the help of a solicitor in order to purchase a property. As it happens, conveyancing isn't at all difficult, particularly if you are buying a freehold house. But if you were the type to go it alone you wouldn't have bought our book, so let's just take it for granted that you are going to employ a professional.

Prepared purchasers instruct a solicitor before they find their new home. Doing this can save time further down the line. Yet again we find ourselves suggesting that you turn to estate agents for advice. They will know which firms in their area are speedy and efficient and those solicitors who only turn to their pile of contracts at 4 p.m. on Friday after a boozy lunch. Ask family and friends for recommendations, but try to stay local. It's all very well using a family lawyer, but familiarity with the area in which you are purchasing your home counts for a lot. Sometimes when clients come to us they already have a solicitor. It is then down to us to train him or her in our little ways. This can be hard going; one legal professional, when asked for her email address, told us with pride that although she did have one she only looked at it 'once in a blue moon'. If the solicitor you are thinking of instructing takes this sort of attitude, don't touch them with a barge pole.

> **PHIL'S TOP TIP**
>
> **Once you find the home of your dreams the only way to hold on to it is by micro managing your purchase. This means constantly keeping a beady eye on everything and everyone concerned with your purchase and move, and never assuming that they are just getting on with it.**

Well done! You've done a great deal of research and hard work and are well on the way to completing your search brief. You have a good sense of what you want and what you can afford.

But, whatever your budget, there are always compromises to be made. For example, if location is your number one priority – the non-negotiable – then you might find you have to compromise on other parts of your brief. We had a client on *Location Location Location* who had very specific requirements. She wanted to be in one particular postcode, near an upmarket supermarket and in the catchment area for a certain school. Phil and I found a house that ticked every box: right location, right size, it was perfect except for the fact it was a bit of a brute to look at. When we pulled up outside the property our lovely client refused to get out of the car and sat in the driveway crying. She has now been living there happily for years. The point is, you can change how a house looks from the outside, but you can't pick it up and move it to a new location. A house is like a face: a bit of mascara and some lippy can do wonders for your appearance. Similarly, new sash windows and rendering over pebbledash can transform the exterior of a house.

KIRSTIE SAYS

"If some of you are thinking, 'Huh, I bet she doesn't stick to her own advice,' you would be wrong. I live in a house in west London which was built post World War Two in a style known as 'Brutalist'. It is constructed from poured concrete so it is next to impossible to change the internal layout because of the thickness of the walls, and the ceiling height isn't great. It is a brute of a building, softened slightly by ivy, but it wouldn't win any prizes for beauty. Why do I live there? Location. The house leads straight on to a communal garden in one of the nicest streets in London. If it was built in 1870, like some of the neighboring properties, it would be out of my budget. See, it is all about compromise."

Now is the time to ask yourself some tough questions. It's a case of what you can and can't achieve. If being in the perfect location is your number one priority and your budget is fixed then what can give? You may have to compromise on space, but if that just isn't possible you will have to consider shifting areas.

3

LOVE ACTUALLY – MEETING THE AGENTS

We've already talked about loving your agents, but it's at this stage that you have to head out on to the high street and put it into practice. You've done your homework, established where you want to live and how much you can afford to spend, so you are way ahead of the game. Now is the time to set out confidently, all the time keeping in mind your search brief.

There is nothing in the world agents like more than prepared purchasers – there are so many time-wasters. As we've said before, you have to stand head and shoulders above the rest to find and secure your dream home, and that's exactly what all this preparation and study has achieved. You are now a prepared purchaser. Agents call buyers applicants, and you are an applicant who knows exactly what you are doing, what you want to buy, what you have to spend and where you are going to spend it.

SUNDAY BEST

Take half a day off work midweek, dress up in your Sunday best and visit all the agents in the area you want to move to.

Prepare house-hunting business cards that have all your contact info plus a brief outline of your requirements. *Do not* hand over your entire search brief – too many details will make you look fussy. Choose those that are most important to you. For example:

- budget

- bedrooms

- minimum reception size

- additional requirements, i.e. outside space, parking, transport links, etc.

Give this card to the agents you meet and take their cards. As you leave scribble some reminder notes for yourself on the card – 'tall, dark and handsome' or 'the one with the mullet'. Anything which means that when you meet them or they ring you up, you will be able to link the name to the face and establish a rapport.

Name:	**Philip & Fiona Spencer**
Current address:	Craven Cottage, Plympton, Kent
Contact details:	Phil 07893 123456 philspencer@home.co.uk Fiona 07894 234567 fionaspencer@home.co.uk
Budget:	£475,000

Finance:	Deposit/equity £190,000
	Lloyds TSB mortgage agreed
	£285,000
Requirements:	5-bedroom period house in rural
	location.
Locations:	Within a 10 mile radius of
	Sevenoaks in Kent.
Outside space:	A big garden will be a key
	motivator.
General:	Looking for a well-balanced family
	house. Happy to redecorate, but
	don't want to do structural
	alterations. Large informal family
	kitchen leading on to decent
	garden is an important element.
Bonus:	Private parking.

Name:	**Kirstie Allsopp**
Current address:	46 Campden Grove, W8 4QP
Mobile number:	07784 548729
Budget:	£450,000
Mortgage agreed:	HSBC
Deposit:	£90,000
Requirements:	4-bedroom house
Locations:	Kensal Rise, Queen's Park, Maida
	Vale, Ladbroke Grove, White City
Use of rooms:	3 double bedrooms, fourth
	bedroom for use as study. I work
	from home a few days a week.

Outside space:	Garden essential for children and dogs – minimum length 35ft.
Additional requirements:	Ideally a large eat-in kitchen and large family bathroom.
Condition of property:	Very willing to do work, actively looking for property with opportunity to add value by extending into loft space available or side return BUT no additional budget available, work levels must be reflected in price.
Compromises:	If the garden was large enough to contain a small shed/wooden home office I would consider a three-bedroom property.
Solicitor:	Tom Sutherland at Price Sutherland 0207 730 1234.

HOT BUYERS' LIST

Make a list of your top ten agents based on how helpful/positive/responsive they were when you visited their offices. Then call all the agents on the list twice a week; don't call at lunchtime (you may not think they are human but they have to eat), or after 4 p.m., as this is when they are most likely to be out on viewings. Try to make sure that you actually speak to your contact – keeping up the relationship is vital. Don't ever expect agents to call you back, you must chase them; loving agents doesn't mean you can expect miracles. Although the business cards you get from agents may have email addresses on them, don't forget that they spend the majority of their time out of the office. Most of the agents we deal with don't do that much work via email, certainly not in the initial stages. Later on, email can be a great help in micro managing your purchase, but that's a long way off yet. Be cheery when you ring and help them to remember you – 'Hi Matt, it's Claire, I came in last week. I was just ringing to see whether you've got anything new on.'

There is a common misconception that estate agents should advise every one of their applicants of every vaguely suitable property that becomes available. It wouldn't matter what the product was, a busy sales rep won't feel the need to make fifty calls if the same result can be achieved in five. Your aim is to ensure that you're number one on that list of five – the hot buyers' list.

> **Try to make sure that you actually speak to your agent – keeping up the relationship is vital.**

A TO Z

When agents do mention something they think you should view, be aware that they may have viewing targets to meet and will want to show you as many properties as they can. Don't move a muscle until you've grabbed your map or A–Z. This is the number one most important tool of the house-hunter – have one at home, one in the office, and one in your car or bag. You've already marked on it the streets/areas you like and those that you don't, when you did your homework. Don't be too rigid on this point, but make the agent aware that you know the area. Pinpoint the property he is talking about on the map and then ask the following:

KIRSTIE SAYS

"Now I can hear some of you saying, 'Who uses A to Zs these days?' Yes, most of us have maps on our smartphones, but the easiest way to clearly see your whole search area in one go is still on a paper map. Also, if you are looking in an area with patchy mobile phone reception, you don't want to find you are lost and late for your viewing because your smartphone isn't working and you don't have a map."

KEY QUESTIONS

Ask him to 'walk you round' the property, i.e. give a room-by-room description. If he hasn't seen it, don't be too hard on him; hopefully your relationship is such that he has rung you the second there is a sniff of this property coming on the market. But at the same time he should be familiar with all his 'stock'. Ask to speak to a colleague who has seen it or, if he is familiar with the street, continue with the other questions.

What is on either side, opposite and behind the property? Again, look on the map for indications of busy roads, railway tracks, schools, hospitals, football stadiums, etc.

What is the downside of the property? (Even Buckingham Palace has a downside.) A good agent is an honest agent and one who realizes that forewarned is forearmed, so encourage him to tell you the good and the bad.

What is the position of the vendors? Why are they selling? Have they found somewhere to go? Are they working to a specific timetable or in a chain? Arguably this question can be left till later, but *don't* forget it, and never ask a vendor why they are moving – they are unlikely to tell you the whole truth.

If it is important to you, ask how far the nearest station or bus stop is. Tell the agent you will be travelling to the property on public transport, so if he is telling porkies about the time it takes to walk from the station to the house he's going to be waiting around! Usually, you are, of course, super punctual for appointments with agents; it's the fast track to their good books.

If you are viewing a property having been sent some written details, don't forget these questions. Keep your wits about you and ask yourself what's missing from the details. Why doesn't it say which direction the roof terrace faces or what the measurements of the garden are? Do you really think the agent would fail to mention that the terrace is 10 feet x 20 feet and south facing? No, we don't think so either. If a flat's on the fourth floor and the details don't mention a lift, believe us, it won't have one. Conversely, be wary of terms like 'at best' or 'max'. Why are they there? Because an agent will want to squeeze in every available foot, but four feet of that space may be under the eaves or in a bay window.

> **PHIL'S TOP TIP**
>
> **It's best to try to see something before the weekend as that's when everyone else will be viewing. If it's right for you, move fast.**

Too many questions and the agent will start to lose the will to live, but the point of all this is to make sure that when you actually view a property there is a reasonable possibility, more than a 50 per cent chance, that it is the one for you.

We do not run around like headless chickens viewing everything that has a 'For Sale' sign outside and nor should you – let your fingers do the walking. Be as flexible as possible with the agent regarding viewing times. If you are seeing different flats with different agents leave yourself time to get from one appointment to the other.

4

VIEWINGS

So you've sneaked out of the office early and you're now standing outside a property waiting for the agent. Worst-case scenario: an agent you don't recognize arrives fifteen minutes late with the wrong set of keys and you want to pour cold coffee into the radiator of his flashy car. Don't! Count to ten, listen to his explanation, ignore the fact that so far the word 'sorry' hasn't been uttered and concentrate on the viewing. Always use any time you spend waiting outside a property on a good look round.

BE EAGLE-EYED

Look at the neighbouring houses:

- Are they well kept up and tidy?

- Are there people in the street having work done? Can you see skips, scaffolding, etc?

- Is the house you're seeing the tidiest in the street or the scruffiest?

- How does the brickwork look? What's the condition of the windows, the roof, the guttering?

- How much parking is there?

- Listen for noise, both human and automobile.

- Who is coming and going?

Review the questions you asked the agent on the telephone. Was he being economical with the truth when answering?

KIRSTIE SAYS

"If you are viewing a flat and the building is scruffy and badly looked after – no proper arrangements for the dustbins, neglected front area and tired common parts (that rather unfortunate phrase is the name for the stairs and corridors in a conversion or block of flats) – then this could be an indication of a rogue landlord, or freeholders who aren't prepared to pay for, or simply take no interest in, the upkeep of the building. If, once you've viewed the flat, you are interested in it, make sure you bully the agent to give you the details of the managing agents and talk to the other residents of the building. Do as much research as you can before spending a penny on surveyors' or lawyers' fees."

GETTING YOUR HOOKS IN

Although it is important not to seem too fussy when giving your requirements to an agent, he does need enough information to enable him to get a grip on your needs. Agents call this information 'hooks', and it's a very good way of ensuring the agent understands what you want *and* remembers it. So don't, for example, just tell the agent you need a garden. Explain to him you need a garden because you've just acquired a lovely Border terrier. Or your partner's done a course in garden design. Or whatever your reason is for wanting a garden. Explain what use each bedroom will have and fill the agent in on your hopes and dreams for this house. Without going over the top, the more vivid you make the details for the agent, the more he understands about you and the way you lead your life. And the closer he will get to finding you the right thing. Do bear in mind, though, that however vivid a picture you paint, an agent can only show you what he has on his books, whereas a home search agent can present you with a selection of everything that is on the market (and that will be our first and last plug for the industry we work in).

ESSENTIAL TOOLS

1. **House-hunting notebook** in which you list all the houses you've seen. Some properties are on with a number of

different agents and particularly in metropolitan areas you can end up arriving to see a house that you've already viewed. In this notebook you can list questions for the agent so that if you do an unaccompanied viewing you remember what to ask when you talk to him afterwards. You can also make your own list of the pros and cons of each property – very useful if there comes a day when you are torn between two different properties.

2. Tape measure and measurements of your key pieces of furniture. The tape measure is not for checking up on the estate agent's details! It's for seeing whether the rooms will accommodate your furniture and whether it will fit into your new home – measure your bed, sofa, dining table, etc. Have these measurements handy in your notebook, and then you'll know from the outset whether this property is suitable. *But* please, please bear in mind that it is madness to base a decision which involves possibly hundreds of thousands of pounds on a single piece of furniture, unless it's a real family heirloom. A client once turned to us and said, 'This kitchen won't do, my new fridge won't fit.' The fridge in question had been bought just a week before the house-hunt began. A £300 fridge versus a £90,000 house – you do the maths. The solution? We suggested the fridge went back to the shop and that a new one was purchased that suited the kitchen.

3. Torch for looking into dark corners, particularly lofts. Perhaps more useful on your second, more detailed viewing.

4. Compass. Most smartphones have a built-in compass but if you wouldn't be parted from your 1999 Nokia brick for all the tea in China you will need to bring a real compass. This is for checking up on agent details.

THE SUN WILL COME OUT TOMORROW

Why does it matter which way a house faces? It's very simple – we live on an island which can be pretty cold and dark half of the year, therefore we need to make the most of any available sun. A house in which the principal rooms face south will always be sunniest. In an ideal world we would all have light in our bedrooms as we got up and the sun in our gardens as we sat sipping a drink after work, but what if you work nights and need to sleep in the day and perhaps you would prefer the sun in your kitchen in the morning as you make a cup of coffee, and if every property in the nation was south facing . . . ? Exactly, it's not possible and, what's more, so much relies on decor – a house can be decorated to maximize the amount of available light. Don't get too hung up on which way a house faces, unless you're building it from scratch, and for that you need Kevin McCloud and his *Grand Designs*, not us. The only place where it really matters is in the garden. If you are looking in a built-up area where other buildings block out the sun, visit the property at different times of day and find out when the sun does hit your little patch, because if it never does you have to ask yourself whether it's worth paying for.

KIRSTIE SAYS

"A few years ago we were property hunting for a lady who was seven months pregnant with her first child. She wanted a west-facing garden so she would be able to enjoy a glass of wine and the last rays of sun in the evening. I often wonder how many times she actually managed that glass of wine in the sun? With little ones, your early evenings are spent wrestling them screaming out of baths, cleaning food mess off the kitchen floor and trying to get the *Peppa Pig* theme tune out of your head. By the time you have fallen on your first glass of wine it is usually pitch black outside."

PHIL SAYS

"Fast broadband is now essential for many people for both work and leisure so it is worth finding out if the house you are viewing is in a broadband black spot. If you live in a broadband restricted area, you may not be able to stream movies or download large documents. Speedtest.net is a free download that allows you to test the performance of mobile connection and broadband speeds."

KNOWING WHAT'S OUT THERE

The majority of buyers make up their minds pretty quickly about a property. So if you don't get the right 'feel' from a house, don't spend ages looking round it. But, at the same time, it's rude to say no on the doorstep – it will embarrass the agent and you'll go down as a tactless buyer who upsets vendors.

It's also very important to build up a picture in your own mind of what is and is not available for your budget in your location. So, as you're there, have a quick scoot around.

FEEDBACK

Always tell the agent what you thought about a property. Agents need feedback, first, in order to develop a more detailed picture of what you are looking for and, secondly, they will be under pressure from their clients (the vendors) to keep them updated on viewers' responses to their property. Sadly for vendors, agents are not as honest as they might be on this latter point. Fearing that criticism of the property will be taken personally by the vendor and damage their relationship, agents back away from being frank about the way in which a property is 'displayed'. *How to Sell Your Home* is a whole other book, but if we can sneak in this one piece of advice for vendors: beg the agents to be as honest as possible. They are experts on what sells well and what buyers like and dislike.

But what if this house is the one for you?

Do *not* jump up and down and tell the agent you'll pay whatever it takes or kiss the vendor as you leave. Neither should you pretend to loathe the place in order to put the agent or vendor off the scent. Say nothing in the property, but ask the agent if he could walk you back to your car or simply a little way down the street. Once you are out of sight of the vendor, mention to the agent that you consider it an interesting property and request an appointment to view it again. Or say, 'That's the best of the bunch, can I call you about it when I get home?' All you are doing at this stage is 'expressing an interest'.

> **Always tell the agent what you thought about a property.**

SECOND VIEWINGS

If you are coming back to look at a house for a second time you have already established that it has 'a feel' that you like. Now is the time to whip out your house-hunting notebook and start using all five of your senses: **sight, sound, touch, smell and taste.**

Viewing a property is as much about what to ignore as it is about what to look out for.

What to ignore

Smells. If the pong is dog, cigarettes or worst of all the pungent odour of teenagers or students, then remember that although you may end up having to replace the carpets, it is possible to get rid of these smells. You must also block your nostrils to the seductive scent of flowers, coffee or bread. These are far more dangerous than the most foul smells because they are indications of a wise and canny seller, a creature who will entice you into their lair and make you pay for the clever things they've done to make their home so much more desirable than the cheaper one three doors down. We've been canny sellers in our time and it takes one to know one. But to end on a warning note, don't ignore the smell if it is damp. (If you don't know what damp smells like, leave some wet laundry in the washing machine for a few days; when you pull it out it smells rotten – that's damp!) And be wary of properties next to restaurants – you may visit the property when the establishment is closed and discover too late that when the kitchens are in full swing and the extractor fan is doing its work it's a very different matter.

PHIL'S TOP TIP

Before calling the agent to arrange another viewing, write out a list of questions that you have regarding the property and look at any notes you've made in your house-hunting notebook.

Also refer back to the questions that you asked before viewing the property. Were there any that the agent was unable to answer? This might be a good time to ask him again.

Dated decor. Don't be put off by Artex – the thick, textured paint that was all the rage in the seventies and eighties. It can be sanded down or plastered over. Also ignore woodchip wallpaper, another past fashion which causes an allergic reaction in many buyers, but isn't that hard to remove – it just requires a hired wallpaper steamer/stripper and a huge vat of elbow grease.

The look. Those canny sellers know how easily seduced we all are by other people's lifestyles and we are particularly vulnerable to this when moving house. We all want to keep up with the Joneses and when moving house we are often hoping to move up the ladder in more ways than one. If you're moving because you want to start a family and you view a house with a beautifully decorated nursery it's very hard to regard the property in a detached fashion.

Equally if you're a first-time buyer who fancies himself as quite the lad about town it's very tempting to spend more time looking at the vendor's stereo system and DVD collection than checking out the guttering. A clever vendor will sprinkle a flat with nicely framed photographs of exotic holidays, the odd designer carrier bag and fill the bathroom with posh lotions and potions. We always tell clients selling their homes to invest in a new kettle and toaster; it's amazing how much they tart up an ageing kitchen. So as buyers you must look away. These things are like a Wonderbra – once it comes off the reality can be pretty disappointing.

What NOT to ignore

Noise. One of the main reasons for visiting a property at different times of day is to gauge noise levels from roads, neighbours and local businesses. If you are buying a flat, it's always worth knocking on the doors of the flats above and below the one you are looking at and, if anyone's at home, asking them to walk around a bit and turn on their TV. This will serve two purposes: you'll discover whether there is a noise issue and you'll check out the neighbours. It is as much about having the type of neighbours who will turn the music down if you ask as it is about having thick walls.

PHIL'S TOP TIP

Your second viewing should always be at a different time of day from your original visit. In winter, when most of your house-hunting is likely to be done when it's dark outside, make sure your second viewing is in daylight. In summer, when it is unlikely you will ever see a property after dark, try and make your second viewing as late in the evening as possible. It is not just light levels that alter with the time of day; so do traffic levels and neighbour noise levels.

> **PHIL'S TOP TIP**
>
> **Don't put the vendor on the spot with too many probing questions. Write them in your book and ask the agent afterwards. You need to make a good impression as you may be competing with other buyers. And remember, it's not very enjoyable having troops of strangers looking round your home making comments.**

You should also pay attention to the following:

- Water pressure: turn on the taps in the bathroom.

- Locate the boiler and see if there is a recent service sticker.

- Check that all windows and doors open and close.

- Look up at the ceiling as you enter every room. Cracks in the ceiling do not always mean trouble, but note any you see in your book.

- Check the number of plugs and radiators in every room. (We know of cases where people have unwittingly bought houses that have no central heating – it won't come up on the survey if it isn't there at all.)

And be aware that changes in season and wind direction can make a big difference to noise levels. Find out about the prevailing wind direction as it will carry both noise and odours with it. Bear in mind that leaves fall off trees; while they can be beautiful to look at during the summer, they could be hiding something you'd rather not look at in winter. Leafy trees also have an insulating effect on noise.

If you do have an offer on a house accepted, you are likely to have a survey done. But if you are as observant as possible from day one then nothing in the survey will come as a nasty shock. What's more, the notes you have made in your book may come in very useful further down the line.

KIRSTIE SAYS

"I lived in an Edwardian house that had been converted into two flats – mine was the ground-floor flat. When I viewed the property I introduced myself to Diana, who was my upstairs neighbour and freeholder. It became clear that there had been a number of noise disputes between her and the owner of the flat I wanted to buy. I was a little surprised at this; both Diana and my vendor were well into their fifties and hardly seemed likely to be playing Eminem into the wee small hours of the morning. Further investigation revealed that it was more a clash of personalities than a major noise issue, so I went ahead with the purchase. Even so I took the precaution of lowering the ceiling in my reception room and putting in some sound insulation. Never a completely successful solution because entirely insulating against noise is almost impossible, but at least she never heard when I was sitting up playing my Neil Diamond CDs."

5

JUST JUMP – MAKING AN OFFER

Brilliant! You've found the one. First, don't panic. Don't lie in bed at night imagining all your furniture in the new house, the parties you'll have and how incredibly happy you'll be in your new home. It's too early for all that and you must try to stay as detached as possible. Easy for us to say, I know, but trust us – we've seen thousands of different homes and no property is unique. If you don't get this one, there will be another.

Do be careful who you tell about this property. This may seem a very cynical piece of advice, but folk tend to make major changes in their lives at the same time as their friends, and if your pals are also house-hunting . . . Well, it doesn't bear thinking about!

Do get out your search brief and see how the property you've picked compares with what you thought you wanted – you may be surprised by the differences.

If you are looking at a flat, now is the time to ask the

agent whether they have all the information regarding, for example, the length of the lease, managing agent's fees, sinking fund, etc. If the agent doesn't have any of these details, which is often the case, it's an indication that the vendor is not particularly well prepared for sale. This shouldn't worry you, but just keep in mind that if you get to the stage where your offer is accepted you will have to address these issues up front and there will be even more need to micro manage the conveyancing.

HOW LONG HAS THE PROPERTY BEEN ON THE MARKET?

This is a key question because it is the number-one indicator that the vendor may be prepared to take an offer that is below the asking price. If a house has just come on the market, a low offer isn't going to cut the mustard, but if something's been hanging about for a while then you can be cheekier. Remember, the asking price is exactly that – an asking price. It will have started life as a valuation and then had the vendor's and agent's hopes and dreams added on. Sometimes asking prices aren't much more than what the agent or vendor feels they can realistically get away with whilst still looking you in the eye.

NEGOTIATING

Unless you absolutely have to, avoid playing your best card first. Leave room to manoeuvre. We always prefer to have our first offer rejected – it's a shot across the bows. See what the reaction is and try to get the vendor to make a counter offer.

There are so many factors involved in a property purchase it's impossible to have a fool-proof negotiating method. We've used hundreds of different purchasing tactics. Each purchase is unique, so tailor your negotiations to the individual deal and the people involved. However much we may try to make this a business transaction, human emotions are deeply embedded in the process.

Remember, it's not just price that's up for negotiation – what about exclusivity, time-scales, fixtures and fittings? Work them all into the deal if you can. Levels of emotion and finance will be running high, so be tough, be strong and don't get carried away!

While you should always discuss things in person with the agent, offers are considered more seriously when confirmed in writing. Offer letters should be headed 'Subject to Contract and Survey' and need to outline everything you consider relevant to the deal. Demonstrate how you will fund your purchase and who's working on the legal side. It is much better to have things set out clearly and in writing from the outset.

KIRSTIE SAYS

It has come to our attention that many estate agents are pressuring applicants into using their in-house financial advisers by refusing to forward offers to the vendors until buyers have seen their mortgage adviser. There is a code of practice for residential estate agents, published by the Property Ombudsman (*Code of Practice for Residential Estate Agents, Effective from 1 August 2011*). It clearly states in section 7c:

By Law you must not discriminate, or threaten to discriminate, against a prospective buyer of the seller's property because that person declines to accept that you will (directly or indirectly) provide related services to them. Discrimination includes but is not limited to the following:

Failing to tell the seller of an offer to buy the property

Making it a condition that the person wanting to buy the property must use any other service provided by you or anyone else.

We understand that estate agents want to do the best for their clients by ensuring that the applicant's offer is serious and they have financing in place, but if you have carried out our advice so far they will know you are a prepared buyer. If you feel pressured at any point into seeing an agent's in-house adviser, politely inform them that you are familiar with the code of practice, and by law they must forward your offer onto the seller.

This should be enough to put them back in their box. If not, tell them they'll have me to deal with if they persist.

PHIL'S TOP TIP

Setting asking prices is not an exact science. Don't be a have-a-go-hero – if you think the asking price is low, and you are getting a good deal, don't chance your arm and offer under the asking price. Keep quiet, pay it and be grateful.

SUBJECT TO CONTRACT AND SURVEY

Thursday, 23 September 2014

Peter Carey
Spencer & Lyon

Dear Peter

RE: 41 Powis Crescent, London

Thank you for all your recent help and time.

We are pleased to submit an offer of £420,000 (four hundred and twenty thousand pounds) for the leasehold being offered.

As you are aware, my wife is expecting our first child and in order to make this property suitable we will have to carry out approximately £15,000 worth of renovation works to convert the property to a three-bedroom property. This extra cost is therefore putting considerable strain on our budget.

Having carried out extensive research and taking into consideration current market conditions, we feel that this is a strong offer.

We would be in a position to exchange contracts in ten working days from receipt of full papers and complete as soon as possible thereafter. We understand the vendor has found a suitable property for himself and is keen for a quick transaction, which would suit us. This offer is subject to the property being offered to us on an exclusive basis, no further viewings to be carried out and all marketing to cease.

We are fully committed and serious purchasers. We feel we have reacted quickly and decisively, which is how we would intend to conduct the transaction.

I look forward to receiving a positive response from your vendor.

Yours sincerely
Robert and Florence Crossley

SEALED BIDS

In a competitive market, sealed bids or 'best and final' offers are common. This situation usually arises when more than one asking-price offer is made on a property. However, what you should know is that the property does not necessarily go to the highest bidder, but to the buyer deemed most suitable by the agent, vendor or vendor's solicitor. Therefore it is vital to present yourself as ready to roll.

Your bid should have five parts:

A well-composed letter should contain the following plus enclosures:

1. The figure that you are prepared to pay in words and numbers, e.g. '£93,453.00 (ninety-three thousand, four hundred and fifty-three pounds)'.
2. The name and address of your solicitor. Remember, prepared buyers instruct a solicitor at the outset; the agent knows this and will be suitably impressed.
3. A letter from your mortgage company/financial adviser stating that your borrowing is agreed.
4. A letter from your bank or building society stating that they hold the funds for your deposit.
5. A personal note added to the letter – something about how much you love the property and look forward to living there.

Deciding how much to offer can be tricky. This really is a one-shot chance. Try to detach yourself from your emotions and examine the original asking price. The amount you are willing to pay is a reflection of whether you believe the asking price to be sensible, combined with how much you like, love or need that specific home. When push comes to shove, market forces dictate value – not surveyors, not square-foot calculations and not even comparable evidence. A property is worth what somebody will pay for it.

For a sealed-bid scenario to develop, several people have obviously felt the asking price to be fair. Of course they may be mad, desperate or rich – but at that particular time for that particular property demand is high. Put yourself in the mindset of the other bidders and consider what they might bid. Based on all that you know, try to come up with the top figure that you feel somebody else is likely to offer. Put the maths into perspective by looking at the increased amount as a percentage of the original asking price. Paying £10,000 above an asking price of £125,000 shows a high 8 per cent increase; whereas the same £10,000 on an asking price of £350,000 reflects an increase of only 2.8 per cent.

Give thought to your situation. How upset would you be to lose this property? Are you prepared to lose it over a few thousand pounds? Equally, are you prepared to pay more than it might be worth?

An agent should stipulate the cut-off time by which all bids must be in. If at all possible deliver your bid by hand just before the cut-off point. It's not unheard of for agents within one office to be competing against each other for the applicant with the winning bid. Therefore if your bid is lying around the office a colleague of the negotiator you're dealing with could call and tip off his purchaser regarding the level of your bid. We also recommend that you ask the agent to set a time by which the vendor will have responded to the bids. It's miserable wasting a perfectly good weekend waiting to hear if you've won or lost. Make plans for a night out on the day of your bid; then you can either celebrate your success or drown your sorrows.

KIRSTIE SAYS

"When a friend of ours was involved in a sealed bid she said in her letter that she would be prepared to pay £1,000 more than the highest bid – she got the flat. If you are really desperate to win your bid, this tactic is definitely worth a try.

Phil thinks this tactic is dodgy as hell, and he disapproves of it being included in our book. He reckons that if everyone who buys this book and is involved in a sealed bid uses this tactic, pandemonium will break out!"

GAZUMPING

To gazump is to accept an offer for your property, allow that party to proceed and then accept a higher offer from a third party, thereby gazumping your original purchaser.

Gazumping is a tricky one; whatever advice we give regarding this thorny topic there will be dissenters. If you've been the victim of gazumping you are not going to like what we have to say, but here goes. Whether to gazump or not is entirely the decision of the vendor; as a buyer it is not your problem, unless of course you get gazumped yourself. If you are shown a property already 'under offer' by an agent it is an indication that the vendor is open to higher offers and would therefore consider gazumping. An agent must do as instructed by the client – holding an agent responsible for gazumping is pointless. To be honest, a couple of grand here or there makes precious little difference to the agent's commission and most agents simply want to sell a house as quickly as they can with as little hassle as possible. One of the best reasons to work so hard on being a prepared purchaser is that you are less likely to be gazumped; vendors are far less inclined to dump a really efficient, fast-moving buyer unless the offer they get is considerably more than yours. If you are offering well below the asking price, clearly you are more likely to get gazumped, but the practice is far less common than the press would have us believe.

When you make an offer, ask the agent to demand an exclusive period in which the house will not be shown to any other purchasers. If you have proved to the agent that you have all your ducks in a row he should be open to this idea. A client of ours once made an offer for a property that was for sale through an agent who was notorious for encouraging gazumping. Yup, we know what we said earlier, but there are rogue agents. We had agreed an exclusive period for our client, but didn't trust the agent to adhere to this. We employed a student to spend his days positioned a little distance from the flat, but keeping a watchful eye on it. On the third day he tipped us off that the agent had just arrived and was viewing the flat with an applicant. The agent was called on his mobile: 'You're in the flat, get out now, otherwise we will pull out of the deal immediately!' He never found out how we knew what he was up to, but it gave him an almighty fright and we developed a reputation in the area for using other-worldly powers in the interests of our clients.

Remember, the deal's not done until contracts are signed. Plenty of purchasers pull out as well as vendors reneging on the deal by gazumping you. The agent is paid to secure the highest price possible.

A prepared purchaser is less likely to be gazumped.

REGIONAL DIFFERENCES

You may already know that the property purchase method in Scotland is entirely different from that in the rest of the UK. Scotland has its own legal system and its own laws governing the ownership of property and land. If you are moving from England to Scotland and you want to know more about purchasing a property north of the border, Consumer Focus Scotland has an online guide called Buying and Selling a Home in Scotland, which will guide you through the process.

Many people do not know that there are also subtle but vital regional differences in the UK. Inevitably, if we listed them here we would miss one out, but as a general rule the further north you go the nearer to the asking price you must go. In areas of the north-east, for example, the asking price can indicate the lowest offer a vendor is prepared to take. If you are a first-time buyer or new to an area it's a good idea to ask a few local agents for advice. Obviously it helps if you remember to do this before you find something you're really interested in. Talk to all the agents you come in contact with – they are a gold mine of local information and insight regarding the market in their area so tap into their reserves of knowledge.

WHEN TO JUMP?

Once you've received as much advice as possible – from agents, family and friends, and the woman in the paper shop – you just have to go for it, chance your arm, and hope that your offer is accepted. And that's the easy bit! Once the agent rings and says it's yours, that's when the hard work really starts.

6

HOLDING ON FOR GRIM DEATH

The agent has rung to say your offer has been accepted! Great, that's fantastic; feel free to crack open the bubbly. But make it speedy, because you have only five minutes in which to celebrate. Around one-third of accepted offers never result in completion. There are endless reasons for this, but the majority of them come down to lack of planning on the part of buyers and vendors, a modicum of apathy on the part of solicitors, and a tendency for agents to simply move on to the next thing once an offer is accepted. You've found your dream home; it's your job to ensure that the sale goes through – you can't rely on anyone else to do it.

NO NEWS IS BAD NEWS

The only way to guarantee that you are not one of the 33 per cent who end up losing out is to micro manage your purchase. This means keeping track of what everyone is doing. Never think that no news is good news – poor communication is the biggest deal breaker of them all.

MEMORANDUM OF SALE

The first thing that should happen is that the agent should ask for your solicitor's details so that he can put together a Memorandum of Sale. This is a sheet which lists the name and address of the vendor, his or her solicitor and the same information about you.

Efficient agents get this done immediately and post it out to all concerned but, even so, you must ask your agent to give you the vendor's details over the telephone.

Your new motto is:

Don't wait for the post

1. Call your solicitor, give him all the details, and ask him to contact the vendor's solicitor by email or telephone and say he is eagerly awaiting the contract. Also ask him to begin email contact with the other side. We've already talked about some solicitors' reluctance to use anything other than the Royal Mail. Never underestimate this tendency – old habits die hard. We have known cases in which solicitors have gone days without contacting each other, indulging in some bizarre game of chicken, neither wanting to lose face by being the first to get in

touch. They make teenagers in love look sensible. Ask your solicitor to get back to you with the reaction from the vendor's solicitor to this request, as this will give you an early indication of how prepared your vendor is for sale. If your vendor hasn't yet instructed his solicitor to draw up a contract, you know you've got your work cut out.

2. Contact your mortgage company and give them the following:

- The full address and postcode of the property. If the agent doesn't know the full postcode call the postcode enquiries line: Monday to Friday, 8 a.m. to 4 p.m., 0906 302 1222, or go to their website www.royalmail.com.

- The name, address and telephone number of the estate agent.

- The name, address and telephone number of your solicitor.

What you can do in fifteen minutes will reduce by two weeks the length of time it takes you to exchange.

BE A PAIN IN THE NECK

Let's get one thing straight – you are the customer.

You are paying the solicitor, you are paying the surveyor

and, most of all, you are paying the mortgage company. They are a business like any other, and it is their business to provide loans. Think of all the other 'big ticket' items you buy – would you take any mucking around from a car salesman or the shop where you bought your sofa? No, so don't accept any from your mortgage company. They've already agreed to lend you the money. So you've got over the first hurdle, and, unless there is something very wrong with the property you intend to buy, they are not going to turn round and say, 'Actually, we've decided we're not right for each other, so, sorry, but we're keeping the money.'

We are not suggesting that anyone should be rude, stroppy or aggressive, just *firm*. Make it very clear from the outset that you are working to a timetable; there are so many unknowns, especially if you are in a chain, that you do not want hitches caused by your workforce.

MICHAEL FLATLEY

This is the point at which the agent will start asking you about a survey. This is a key stage in the proceedings, so listen up because our take on this is a bit different from the norm.

All along you've been working to prove to the agents and vendors that you are a prepared purchaser, able to jump forward and execute the purchase of your dream home in seconds; momentum is your watchword – you've learned that it's essential to keep everyone on their toes and leaping around like the cast of *Riverdance*. So it's going to seem very strange to read that this may be the moment to put the brakes on, but do *not* have a survey done just yet.

THE METER'S RUNNING

Thus far you have incurred very few costs: you will have paid a mortgage arrangement fee, perhaps taken some time off work, and have spent more money on petrol and phone bills than usual, but this house-hunting lark hasn't set you back much. Once you start having regular correspondence with your solicitor and there's talk of a survey, the meter's running.

THE ACID TEST

Estate agents don't rest easy until a survey has been done. They regard this as the acid test; it proves to them that the buyer is up to speed and committed to the purchase. Remember, there are a lot of time-wasters out there who are the bane of any agent's life. In many ways the agents are right – a survey costs money and flaky purchasers will fall at this hurdle. But we are here to help buyers and our concern is to protect you from flaky sellers.

Do not wait until the agent asks you when the survey is going to be done. Inform him at the start that although everyone is ready to go and you have passed on all the details of the property to your lender, you will not proceed with the survey until your solicitor has received the draft contract or until he is satisfied that it is well on its way. A survey can be arranged and conducted in as little as forty-eight hours, and this practice prevents you from wasting your money. There is nothing more frustrating than spending hundreds of pounds on surveys and lawyer's fees only to discover that the vendor was just testing the water and never really intended to sell the property, or was simply using you as a stalking horse, a tool to encourage higher offers, intending to gazump you if they received any.

Don't forget to discuss this 'contract before survey' policy with your solicitor. He must be kept informed of any tactic or negotiating tool.

GO EASY

Be gentle with the agent on this matter – it will unnerve him – but stick to your guns. There are two further reasons for taking this tack. First (and this is most relevant to buyers of flats), if your solicitor has a quick look at the lease before a survey is carried out, he will be able to inform you of any hurdles, such as dogs being prohibited, service charges beyond your budget or a ban on subletting. Secondly, your solicitor can also supply the surveyor with a copy of the floor plan/boundaries of the flat. This is part of the contract and if it doesn't bear any resemblance to the current layout of the property will reveal whether any major alterations have recently been made to the building. Your solicitor will therefore know to ask the vendor for the district surveyor's certificate and your surveyor will be able to pay special attention to the standard of any alterations; for example, if any walls have been removed, whether the floors and ceilings have been properly supported.

As with everything, if you are proactive and always two steps ahead of the game, you will build 'momentum' and keep the whole process steaming along. Your train is currently at an orange light just outside the station.

PHIL'S TOP TIP

Get three sets of details for the property you are buying. Send one to your solicitor and two to your lender (they should hold one set for their own records and pass the second on to the surveyor).

Your solicitor will then be able to compare the details to those on the fixtures and fittings list – a document you will soon become all too familiar with. Your mortgage company is bound to ask for the details at some stage, and it will impress them if you are prepared.

KIRSTIE SAYS

"When I moved into my flat it had two bedrooms, a tiny bathroom and kitchen, and a reasonable-size sitting room. It now has one bedroom, a generous bathroom and a

large open-plan kitchen diner/sitting room. The floor plan is therefore entirely changed and when I come to sell my flat I will provide the buyer's solicitor with the following:

1. District surveyor's certificate – this is from my local authority surveyor, and it means he has approved my alterations and ensured that they adhere to appropriate safety regulations.

2. Structural engineer's plans – this explains where the RSJs (the huge metal beams which support the areas above the walls I removed) are, and how they were fitted.

3. A copy of the original architect's plans for my alterations.

All this will reassure my buyer that the work was done properly."

Tips for sellers are as rare as hens' teeth in this book, but if you are selling it really pays to get all your paperwork together before you even think of instructing an estate agent. When you first consider selling, your number one call should be to your solicitor; ask him to get out the contract you received when you purchased the house, dust it down, and get everything together. This guarantees that when you accept an offer from a bright-eyed, bushy-tailed, prepared purchaser who has read this book from cover to cover the whole process will be a walk in the park.

SURVEYS

If all is well and the contract has arrived at your solicitor's office, you can race ahead with the survey.

There are three types of survey:

1. The valuation survey

This involves the surveyor visiting the property, taking a quick look and ringing estate agents in the area to get 'comparables'. Essentially this is an attempt to ensure that the price you intend to pay for the property is reasonable. Your mortgage company is not going to lend you the money if they think you're paying massively over the odds, because if you're run over by a bus the day after completion they won't get their money back.

2. The homebuyer's survey

This involves both a valuation and a more thorough look around, checking out the boiler, electrics, brickwork, etc. It will flag up any problem areas that might need fixing or maintaining. The surveyor is likely to recommend a more detailed inspection.

3. A full structural survey

This is the full monty. While a homebuyer's survey will tell you what's wrong, a full structural survey will tell you what's wrong, why it's wrong and what you should do about it.

> ### PHIL'S TOP TIP
>
> **In an ideal world you would accompany the surveyor to the property. The reason for this is that while he may need to be very cautious and conservative when writing out his report, a friendly surveyor will often give a quick verbal report which may be just as informative. We've often had on-site chats with surveyors in which they've said, 'I'll be mentioning x or y in my report, but it looks pretty sound and I reckon this is a good buy.'**

If you are buying a flat, particularly in a large block, or a newly built house, a full structural survey may be an unnecessary expense. In the case of flats, unless a surveyor can get access to every flat in the building, the roof and the basement, a structural survey cannot really be complete.

Your mortgage company will usually require a survey. Although they will arrange it, you will be charged for the survey. If you have a particular surveyor you want to use, do give it a try. But most lenders have their own panel of surveyors whom they rely on.

At this stage refer back to your house-hunting notebook. Did you make any notes which should be passed on to the surveyor? Did you have any questions regarding cracks or bulges in walls or ceilings? Are you interested in making any structural alterations to the flat about which the surveyor might be able to give you advice? Make sure you pass on as much information as possible to the surveyor;

he doesn't have bionic eyes and two pairs of eyes are better than one. If you've both had a good look over the property there is far less likelihood of any problem being overlooked.

We have never, ever seen a 100-per-cent-OK survey; surveyors highlight problems, they do not highlight plus points. If you weren't able to accompany the surveyor to the property and you then receive a report which troubles you, don't be afraid to give the surveyor a ring. Again, he may be less formal on the telephone and give you his off-the-record feelings on the property. Tell him your budget, level of experience, and how much work you intend or don't intend to do. Surveyors, like estate agents, view hundreds of different properties every year, so make use of their knowledge and experience. After all, you're paying the bill.

One final point: mortgage companies do not lend money to buy ropey houses. You'll soon know what constitutes a major problem on the survey because your mortgage company will pick up on it.

During these early days after the acceptance of your offer you will want to discuss a timetable with the estate agent. When might we be exchanging? When do the vendors wish to complete? This is the point at which you may become horribly familiar with . . .

PHIL SAYS

"As we have said throughout this new book, lenders have become more cautious. You might think that the hard bit is over – you have your 'agreement in principle', now it's just a matter of your mortgage provider carrying

out the valuation survey and lending you the said amount. Unfortunately, there seems to be a growing trend of down-valuation – overly cautious surveyors under-valuing properties. If this happens you can appeal a valuation and the best thing to do is provide details of three similar properties that have sold in the local area. Sadly, if your appeal is not upheld you will be forced to go back to square one and look elsewhere for a mortgage offer."

THE PROPERTY CHAIN

If you are a first-time buyer, buying a brand-new house from a developer, we've got good news for you – you can skip this section. For the rest of you, hang on in there because this bit really matters. A property chain occurs when more than one house is involved in the transaction and it is probably best explained thus:

Rob Younge
First-time buyer, nothing to sell, wanting to buy a one-bed flat.

Flora Baxter and Rory Kinley
Flora is selling her one-bed flat and moving in with her boyfriend, Rory. They are buying a two-bed maisonette in the same city.

Miranda Rose and James Miller

Young couple selling their two-bed maisonette and buying a three-bed house with a garden. The commute to work will be longer but their new rescue dog needs outside space and they are hoping to start a family soon.

Sophie and Paul Alan

Sophie and Paul have two young kids and another on the way. They are fed up with urban living and want to move to the countryside. Sophie dreams of a vegetable patch and some chickens and sending her two eldest to the nice primary school in the village.

Susan and Brian Fletcher

Susan and Brian have both recently retired and are moving to Australia to be closer to their son, John, his Australian wife, Ellen, and their two grandchildren. They are selling their four-bed cottage on the edge of Exmoor.

You still with us?

Now, here's where it gets tricky, because if anything goes wrong with any of these transactions it has a knock-on effect on the whole group. If Flora and Rory decide they've been too hasty and maybe should rent first as they've only been going out for six months, or if Miranda and James get a survey done which says that Sophie and Paul's roof needs to be replaced and they can't afford that added expense, the whole thing comes down like a pack of cards.

You can do everything in your power to be a well-prepared, knowledgeable buyer, yet your dream home can be whipped away from you because someone you've never met, selling a house 300 miles away, is told that her daughter is expecting a baby and suddenly decides that living in France is not such a good idea.

All you can do is follow our advice, make sure you're all ship-shape and hope that everyone in your chain is also reading this book.

7

PUSH, PUSH, PUSH

So far so good. With any luck by this stage you have had an offer accepted, your solicitor has received a contract from the vendor's solicitor, and you have had a survey carried out.

But if these things haven't happened, don't despair. Micro managing is as much about knowing what is *not* happening as about knowing what *is* happening. What if it is two weeks since your offer was accepted and so far no contract has arrived at your solicitor's office?

TACTIC ONE

Start by asking your solicitor to ring the vendor's solicitor and ask directly why the contract hasn't been forthcoming. Remember, solicitors don't like the telephone very much so be very clear on this point. The most common delay at this stage is caused by a failure on the part of vendors to prepare properly for sale. One thing that holds up delivery of the contract is not having the deeds. These are the pieces of paper that prove ownership of a property and are usually held by the vendor's mortgage company.

If you are selling a property, one of the first things you should do is contact your mortgage company. Inform them of the situation and ask them to send the deeds of the property to your solicitor.

Most vendors fail to do this, and most mortgage companies take up to twenty-eight days to send the deeds through; until the solicitor has the deeds he cannot send out a full and legal contract. If the deeds are what is holding up the proceedings it is likely that the vendor's solicitor will admit this to your solicitor, but if there seems to be no adequate explanation for the delay and your solicitor senses that the other side is stalling, you must move on to your next tactic.

TACTIC TWO

If you solicitor has been unable to uncover a reasonable excuse for the delay, call the estate agent. Unless you buy this property the agent doesn't get paid and he has to start marketing the property all over again. Therefore he wants you to get this house almost as much as you do. The only thing is that mentally he has moved on – he's concentrating on the houses that aren't under offer. Tell the agent that you have not yet received a contract and that when your solicitor called the vendor's solicitor he could give no explanation for the delay.

As always, be friendly and polite. By now you're old friends and he is as much on your side as he will ever be. Explain that although you love the property you have offered on, you may be forced to start looking at other things, as it seems the vendor isn't really that keen on selling.

Don't go overboard with this tactic, but bear in mind that at this point the agent will be thinking, 'Oops, what happens if they find something they like more and withdraw from the purchase?' This is quite possible, as you are not in any way obligated to buy the property you've made an offer on. Arguably you should go on looking at other properties regardless of how your purchase is proceeding. The case against doing this is that it's a remarkably small world and if it gets back to your vendor that you are still house-hunting, despite having made an offer for his property, he might decide that if you're still looking, he can keep showing. Therefore you run a greater risk of being gazumped.

Once you have given the agent a little shove, he will give the vendor a little shove who, in turn, will give his solicitor a little shove and things should get going. If this doesn't happen, carry out your threat and restart your search. This is no time for a head-in-the-sand approach.

LEASEHOLD PROPERTIES

If you are buying a freehold house, the good news is that you can skip this bit. But if you are buying a leasehold house or flat, or a property with a share of the freehold, then listen up.

There is enormous confusion surrounding leasehold and share of freehold and, frankly, it's hardly surprising. Every week arcane, unintelligible leases arrive on our desks, at which point we stop mouthing off on the subject of the legal profession's inability to communicate in the modern world and pray that they know what they are doing, because half the time we can't make head or tail of what we are looking at.

The whole concept of leasehold is a difficult one to grasp. You are expected to hand over thousands and thousands of pounds, mortgaging yourself to the hilt in order to obtain the Holy Grail of home ownership. But then it turns out that you won't own the property at all, you'll just be renting it for a very long time and, like all tenants, you will be handed a long list of rules and regulations and in some cases the time you're renting for isn't half long enough. As a client of ours said recently when we were discussing his short lease, 'I may still be alive in forty-eight years' time!'

A layman's definition may help: a leasehold property, more often a flat than a house, is one that is effectively rented for a long period of time, anything from ten to 999 years. What you are buying is the lease, which is the right to rent the property. The flat remains the property of the freeholder, to whom, in most cases, you pay an annual ground rent. This is often referred to as a 'peppercorn rent' as it is usually a nominal amount, for example £25.

No two leases are exactly the same, and your solicitor's job is to scrutinize the lease in order to establish that everything is in order. He is responsible not only to you, his client, but, very importantly, to your mortgage company, who rely on the opinion of both the surveyor and your solicitor to judge the suitability of the property. The mortgage company won't agree to lend you the money until they have got the OK from both of them.

One of the things your solicitor has to establish is whether the flat is in a properly maintained building, and it is at this hurdle that many transactions fall. Rogue freeholders who fail in their responsibilities to their tenants are the bane of our lives. Depending on the wording of the lease, generally landlords are responsible for the upkeep of their buildings: the brickwork or painting, the interior decoration of the common parts, the roof, etc. But – and this is a very important point – they are not responsible for paying for this work; this is down to the tenants. As with anything to do with property, when it comes to leasehold agreements use your nous (and a good solicitor), and you won't go far wrong.

WHAT IF

This is the stage at which any number of problems can arise: structural, financial or legal. However long our list of potential hiccups, you can bet that your particular problem won't be included, so best that we don't try! What we can do is offer a few wise words which cover a multitude of sinners.

Much as we may mock solicitors for their old-fashioned ways, it is important to realize that what you're paying them to do is to protect you from purchasing a property which may turn out not to be what you thought it was. At some stage you have to put yourself in their hands and trust that they know what they are talking about. If there has been anything about their professional conduct which has concerned you, do not hesitate to get a second opinion. But solicitors are like any other professional; the majority know what they are doing and rogue ones are rare.

If a problem crops up which the solicitor wants to double-check, the estate agent is bound to grumble and say things like, 'Well, it wasn't a problem for the current owner; your solicitor is just being picky.' Listen to what he is saying, but take it with a pinch of salt. Agents often think solicitors are being too fussy. The important thing is to make sure that your solicitor raises any queries with the other side as swiftly as possible. If the agent makes a more strongly worded complaint about your solicitor do not take it personally – a mistake that buyers and sellers often make; instead ask yourself whether his comments confirm any fears you've already had.

WHAT IF NOT?

In the end your solicitor will advise you either to go ahead with the purchase or not. Is it the end of the line if your solicitor says that, in his opinion, he does not think you should proceed with the purchase?

Yes (maybe). We have, on occasion, suggested that a client go against the advice of their solicitor, but this is the exception not the rule. In many cases, if your legal adviser isn't happy your mortgage lender won't be either. There is no doubt that solicitors will always err on the side of caution and if torn between a 'yes' and a 'no' they are more likely to go with a 'no'. As with the surveyor, it may be worth having an informal chat and asking your solicitor how close he was to saying yes.

Then ask yourself the following questions:

- Have you a friend or family member who has extensive experience of house buying who you could turn to for advice?

- Was there an estate agent – not the one you are buying from – who struck you as particularly wise and helpful?

- Would you be happy to discuss the problem with the

agent you are buying from? Perhaps he could shed some light on the situation (another large pinch of salt required).

- Would you continue against legal advice if you could negotiate a reduction in your purchase price?

As always, use your common sense.

Don't forget . . . no property is unique; moving on may be the best answer.

OUR SURVEY SAYS . . .

Another major stumbling block can be the survey. Read through it carefully, always remembering that there is no such thing as a perfect survey. If you are not familiar with them, surveys can make alarming reading; you may want to start at the back of the document where the surveyor will have listed or highlighted certain issues. This is a sort of summary of the survey and if nothing particularly alarming is mentioned you can breathe more easily and read on.

KIRSTIE SAYS

"I remember listening to a phone-in show on Radio 4 on my way to view a property once. A lady caller was outraged that on the eve of exchange she had been asked for more money. She explained that the vendor had said that in the 12 weeks between his acceptance

of her offer and the eve of exchange the flat had gone up in value. Strangely the caller's anger seemed, for the most part, to be directed at the estate agent. On hearing this I had to call in. I argued that:

a) The agent was simply the messenger; the decision was entirely the vendor's. No agent in his right mind suggests this idea to a vendor. The amount concerned does not make enough difference to the agent's fee to risk the deal falling apart and all his hard work going down the drain; and

b) Why on earth did it take 12 weeks to exchange? If the delays were caused by the purchaser then I didn't blame the vendor at all for trying it on. It's a risky tactic and not wildly honourable, but when markets are rising swiftly and the vendor knows that if he puts the property back on the market he could get more for it than it's currently under offer at, he may well try to get the best possible price for his asset. It's a sobering tale, but illustrates why pushing forward is essential."

If the surveyor does flag up any issues, the first thing you should do is find out if the situation can be rectified and, if so, how much it's going to cost you. If you intend to do a lot of work to a house, the chances are that you have already been round with more than one builder and the survey only confirms what you already know. But if you thought you were buying a property in pretty good nick and this turns out not to be the case, this is a very different matter.

For example:

The survey says that the roof is in a desperate state of repair and requires immediate attention. The first thing you should do is ask around for a local builder. Again, approach family, friends and agents for a recommendation. Explain the circumstances to the builder and show him a copy of the survey. If he's good and honest, there's every likelihood that he will say, 'Well, if you ask me, that roof's got at least five years of life left, but it might be a good idea to replace a few tiles and redo the flashing. It's not going to cost you a fortune.'

But what if that's not the situation? Let's take a look at the worst-case scenario. The roof needs completely redoing, you have three builders examine the property, and the best estimate for the work is £12,000.

Forward the estimates to your solicitor and discuss your next move with him; we suggest that if you are buying a house which seemed, on the surface of things, to be in perfect order and was priced accordingly, you could now reduce your offer by 50 per cent of the cost of the repairs (in this case, £6,000). If you simply cannot afford to spend a penny on doing any work to the house then you will have to reduce your offer by 100 per cent of the cost of the work. This is slightly unfair on the vendor, as they will, in effect, be paying for the new roof while you will be receiving the benefits. But needs must in some circumstances.

Go carefully, keep it professional, and do not assume that the vendors knew about the condition of their roof (or damp course or bay window or kitchen extension) and kept it under wraps. In our view, though, a good agent should have spotted a dodgy roof and, adopting the attitude forewarned is forearmed, should have let you know about its condition.

KIRSTIE SAYS

"When buying a property, I used to always take Ken to see it long before I had the survey done. Ken is a wise and canny builder I had worked with numerous times. He's seen it all and he often told me straight away whether my plan for knocking down this or that wall was a good idea or not. If you are buying something that you think may throw up problems on a survey or you are considering making alterations, think about paying a builder to have a look around. This way he is not giving up his time for free in the hope of getting a job. He will be able to give you some rough costings for anything you're thinking about doing to the property, and any negatives in the survey will be less of a nasty surprise. Now, I take round my partner Ben (sorry to disappoint anyone who thought I was married to Phil). He is a property developer and there isn't much about houses that he doesn't know. He can tell me pretty much instantly whether a house is in good nick or not and how much it would cost to do any repairs needed."

> **If the surveyor does flag up any issues, the first thing you should do is find out if the situation can be rectified and, if so, how much it's going to cost you.**

The same rules apply to anything else which crops up in the survey – if it was unexpected, if the agent didn't inform you of the problem, and if it is not reflected in the price you agreed, calculate what you can afford to spend plus how much you want this property, then deduct that from the cost of the work and alter your offer accordingly.

Always provide vendors with a copy of the survey and the paperwork from the builders so that they know you have made every effort to get the cheapest estimate and that the figure hasn't been pulled out of thin air. Although you must always keep your solicitor informed, it should be the agent who gently tells the vendor of the reduction in your offer. It always helps to send a letter to your vendor, via the agent, explaining that although you understand that a reduction in your offer is hardly good news, you are still keen to buy the property and hope very much that they will consider your revised offer favourably.

EVERYTHING BUT THE KITCHEN SINK

At this stage you may receive a fixtures and fittings list. This is a standard form filled in by the vendors listing what they intend to remove or leave behind at the property. There are four columns: the first is a list of items and the others are headed 'Included in sale', 'Excluded from sale' and 'None at property'. Sometimes there is an additional column headed, 'Available to purchase'.

Don't let the fixtures and fittings list be a deal-breaker.

You hope that there will be no unpleasant surprises in the list you receive. *But read through it very carefully* because it's no good, when you move in, being furious that the cooker's gone if it stated clearly in the fixtures and fittings list that it was going. A great deal of hassle is caused by this list, and vendor and buyer can become extremely heated. It is a mystery to us how on earth folks can get so agitated over a £275 tumble dryer when they are selling/purchasing a £275,000 house, but believe us, they do. Actually, that's not entirely true, we do know why they get in such a state. It's because at this stage you are so near to doing the deal that you can almost smell it and nerves get frayed as both purchaser and vendor have, by now, spent or committed to spend a considerable amount of money.

PHIL'S TOP TIPS

- **Never use the estate agent's details as anything more than a rough guide as to what's going and what's staying. It is not a legal document and, particularly in cases where less than the asking price has been accepted, vendors often take everything that isn't actual bricks and mortar.**

- **It can be a great help to revisit the property once you have received the fixtures and fittings list. You may not have seen it for three or four weeks and it may be hard to remember some of the items mentioned. Take the agent with you, and make sure he has a copy of the list.**

- **At this stage although information is going back and forth between the solicitors, the agent may be a little in the dark and, as you know, he'll do anything in his power to smooth the sale through. If he thinks the vendors are being unreasonable he may well have a word with them.**

Fixtures and fittings lists become the focus for any niggling resentments about the amount of money you are paying or receiving for the property and a little devil on your shoulder says, 'Flaming hell, I'm paying an arm and a leg for this house; you would have thought they could leave behind the loo seat!' Ignore this little devil; he'll only be happy when he's established squatter's rights on your shoulder and gone on at you so much about this and that, you end up pulling out of the deal altogether. If you are really unnerved about your vendor and his attitude to the house he is leaving behind, then you have the option of a pre-completion check (see page 117) and withholding funds.

This is the stage when you may be able to negotiate to buy certain items, usually white goods such as washing machines or dishwashers. But beware; the relative cost of these products seems to drop all the time and as vendors tend to want a high proportion of what they paid (sometimes as much as 70 per cent) it does not always pay to buy them second-hand. We recently did a deal where the vendor wanted more for a dishwasher than the updated version of that machine was currently selling at.

Remember, your solicitor sees a great many fixtures and fittings lists. Discuss any concerns you have with him, and he'll be able to tell you whether he thinks your vendor is being unreasonable.

Don't let the fixtures and fittings list be a deal-breaker. However much you want that Smeg fridge in duck egg blue it isn't worth risking the sale now.

SAME DAY EXCHANGE AND COMPLETION

When we first wrote this book, simultaneous exchange and completion was very rare. Unfortunately, it has been growing in popularity and in many cases it is a recipe for disaster. The timescale between a normal exchange of contracts and completion varies enormously depending on each sale, but 14–28 days is a good rule of thumb. Simultaneous exchange and completion means you exchange contracts and complete (i.e. receive the keys to your new property) on the same day. The supposed benefits are twofold: as a buyer you do not have to hand over the deposit, and you receive the keys of your new property sooner.

But there are serious pitfalls to this new trend. A sale is not legally binding until you exchange contracts and there is no certainty completion will take place until this point. Either party can pull out prior to exchange and the sale will fall through. The period between exchanging and completion is effectively a safety net, and gives you time to organize your move. For example, councils will usually require at least a week's notice to suspend parking, you will need to give your utility and internet providers ample time to change address, and most removal firms require a deposit to secure a moving date. Even if you have taken a day off work, have your removal team ready to go, had the gas and internet disconnected at your home, and all your boxes packed, unless you have already exchanged contracts you have absolutely NO guarantees you are actually going to complete that day.

As we discussed earlier, most property transactions involve a chain, and it only takes one person in this chain to pull out to bring down the whole house of cards. Your vendor might be keen as mustard to sell and be ready to exchange only for the house they are purchasing to be withdrawn from sale and subsequently your sale falls through too. Or, similarly, there could be a problem your end, for example the monies are not transferred in time and you can't complete. Either way, you will be left out of pocket, sitting amongst a sea of boxes probably weeping into a Chinese takeaway.

Take our advice, play it safe, don't be tempted to cut corners, and resist the temptation to exchange and complete on the same day.

8

GETTING BACK IN THE SADDLE

We know how you feel. It's happened to us, both personally and professionally, and it ain't no fun when a property sale falls through. There was a time when we didn't have the experience we have now and, to be honest, regardless of everything and anything we do, sometimes things still go pear-shaped.

One of a mass of things may have gone wrong. You've been gazumped, lost a sealed bid, had a vendor who got cold feet about selling, been in a chain that collapsed, or it's turned out there was something so wrong with the property that you felt you couldn't continue with the purchase.

This chapter suffers from a bit of an identity crisis because it is about getting back into the market and finding something even better than before, but also about never giving up; your dream home is not 'sold' to someone else until contracts have been exchanged, and that, as you now know, takes time.

> **The very fact that you haven't skipped this chapter means you've almost certainly suffered a bitter disappointment.**

KIRSTIE SAYS

"You're probably sick of hearing about my old flat – the one with the garden for Foxy, and Diana, who lived upstairs (and wasn't loud). But this story may be particularly relevant.

When I first saw that flat I was besotted. Miranda, my old business partner (believe it or not there was life before Phil), was actually the one who spotted it. She came back to the office one day saying, 'I've seen this flat, it needs a ton of work, but there's a shed in the garden with a heart cut in the door and you're going to love it.' Miranda was dead right, but the vendor told me that the lease said no dogs, so before making an offer I felt I had to find out from the freeholder whether I could keep a dog in the flat. She was away for a long weekend, so although I expressed a very strong interest in the flat I didn't make an offer until Tuesday morning, in case I had to subsequently withdraw it. Imagine my horror when I was told the vendor had accepted an offer from someone who had looked round on Saturday.

I was gobsmacked. I thought I had struck up a rapport with the vendor and that at the very least she would have given me an opportunity to match the other offer, but no. And despite my best efforts to gazump, the vendor wasn't having any of it. I went out and looked at other flats, but two or three times a week I rang Angela, the agent, who was selling 'my flat'. 'Have they exchanged yet?' I asked. 'I'm still keen and ready to roll. What's taking so long? Perhaps the other vendor is not as prepared as me?' I was always very relaxed with her, but I wasn't going to let her forget for a moment that I was in the wings. Nine weeks later Angela rang me; the vendor of 'my flat' was fed up with the shillyshallying of her purchaser and if I could exchange within a couple of weeks it could be mine.

Two lessons learned: first, go on and on badgering the agent about your lost love while continuing to look around, but, secondly, never hesitate to put in an offer. I delayed for an honourable reason but it nearly cost me dear.

Take no prisoners; all is fair in love and house buying."

NOT A VERY GOOD PLACE TO START

If you've bought this book after a house-buying mishap and, not surprisingly given its title, you've turned to this chapter first, go back to the beginning. You may still be able to get the house or flat you originally wanted by following our advice, or you may discover that in fact it isn't the right property for you.

INCY WINCY SPIDER

If you have lost a sealed bid, the same applies – don't just walk away. Often in sealed bid scenarios one purchaser gets carried away and catches a touch of competitive fever. They will pay anything just to win. In the cold light of day, and especially if the agent has been unwise enough to tell them how much higher their bid was than the others, winning bidders often start mucking about, picking holes in the property and trying to find ways to shave a bit off what they are paying. Make sure you're there waiting, like a trapdoor spider, ready to pop up and grab the property should the buyers loosen their grip for a single second.

GETTING DUMPED

If your vendor just got cold feet, do walk away. If you've followed the advice in earlier chapters, you will already have done everything in your power to keep the train on the tracks. We all know that when you are dumped by a boyfriend or girlfriend you have to pick yourself up, dust yourself down and get back out there. Many relationship rules apply equally well to house-buying. There is nothing so shocking as discovering that the lover you dropped from a height last month is now shacked up with someone new. You might just find that your vendor comes crawling back, jolted out of their 'I can sell any time I want' attitude by the speed with which you've moved on.

QUESTIONS AND ANSWERS

If you lost your potential new home because of an issue that came up in the survey or a legal complication that your solicitor could not resolve, you have a few questions to ask yourself before moving on.

- Did you overreact to the survey? As we've already said, surveys can be frightening, more so if you are a first-time buyer or have no experience of renovating a property. Did you get a second opinion?

- Did you follow our advice and take a friendly builder to view the property? No flat or house is perfect. Caution is wise, but if you are too risk-averse the biggest risk you run is never finding anything that comes up to scratch.

- Do you still have a nagging feeling that your solicitor was being too conservative? If so, go back to the 'What if' section of Chapter 7 (page 96) and review the problems. If you're still not confident that you were right to give up on 'the one' then get a second opinion.

PLENTY MORE FISH IN THE SEA

But sometimes you can't win, it's gone, and you can't get it back. What now? Get out all your old lists of estate agents' numbers and get on the telephone.

Explain that you haven't been in touch for a while because you found the right property and then explain what happened. Keep it brief. We know it was traumatic but the agent doesn't need a blow-by-blow account; just enough to illustrate that the collapse of the sale was in no way your fault, and you remain a prepared purchaser. Tell the agent which property it was that you intended to buy. If he knows his patch he will be familiar with the street or village and maybe the house itself, and get a better idea of what you are looking for. At the same time, make it clear that you are open to new ideas, and realize that hoping to find an exact replica of your 'lost love' would be foolish.

It is hard at this stage to see the silver lining in the cloud, but it has been our experience that there invariably is one. It just isn't immediately obvious. In a year's time when you are happily ensconced in your new home, you will think, 'Imagine if we'd got that first house we made an offer on. This is so much better.'

9

PREPARING FOR
THE BIG DAY

Well done, congratulations, you've exchanged contracts! This means that, without a doubt, you will get your mitts on the property you've worked so hard to find. At this stage people's experiences diverge widely – many of you may have to complete at the same time as you exchange, or within twenty-four or forty-eight hours of exchange, while others will have a more manageable period in which to sort things out.

We hope that if you are in the former group you will have decided to read this chapter prior to exchange, otherwise you'll be up all night desperately trying to put into place 'Our successful move strategy' (see page 119). Rapid exchange and completion often occur if you are involved in a chain which overshoots its proposed exchange date, but attempts are made to stick to the original completion date – the gap between the two narrows and this can make life very difficult. You have to plan ahead, book removal men, etc. without any guarantee that the purchase will take place. Talk to the estate agent and explain that you are now making arrangements which cost money. Ask him to be as honest as he can about the likelihood of everything coming together, and not to do anything that you cannot undo.

TAKING IT EASY

If you are fortunate enough to be living with parents or friends or renting a room on an informal basis, all the tension of a rapid exchange and completion is removed.

You do not have a date on which you must move out and therefore can move in at your leisure, even if you have weeks between exchange and completion. Not having to move all on one day, on the heels of the previous owner, is a huge luxury. Of course, everyone is anxious to get started in their new home but if, for example, your proposed completion date is on a Friday, set your mental move-in date as Sunday. Being able to move in slowly is a very rare treat. It's not possible if you are moving far from home or if you have been renting on a more formal basis and have had to give your landlord a month's notice, but the joy of hanging pictures, assembling cupboards and, of course, scrubbing every surface while still being able to go back to your own bed at night, cannot be overstated.

SHOCKING STATE OF AFFAIRS

What never fails to surprise us is the state people leave their houses in, fixtures and fittings aside. Brace yourself for a shock when you first walk into your new home. Anyone with any sense keeps everything up to scratch while the property is being marketed, but a great many people let it all go once the deal's been done. For many people it is simple good manners to have a go with the Hoover and clean the bathroom, to give the lawn one last mow and to leave, at the very least, light bulbs and loo roll behind. Some kind souls leave flowers or a bottle of bubbly in the fridge and we have gone to pick up keys on our client's behalf and found owners on their hands and knees cleaning out the space behind the fridge. But sadly this is by no means always the case. Expect the worse, and arm yourself with quantities of cleaning items. (Mothers tend to be the most useful, but prepare yourself for constant exclamations of, 'How can people live like this?'!)

PRE-COMPLETION CHECK

Leaving behind a mucky house is one thing; irritating but easily sorted with a bit of elbow grease. But if you have any reason to fear that your vendor may damage the property while moving out or may not intend to abide by the fixtures and fittings list, then you may want to discuss a pre-completion inspection with your solicitor. Just the threat of this is enough to make most vendors pull their socks up; many people are unaware that a house must be in the same condition on completion as it was on exchange.

A pre-completion inspection simply involves you and the estate agent having a quick look around the house before you authorize your solicitor to hand over the money, but everyone needs to know in advance that this will happen. It is tricky to organize because, particularly if you are in a chain, you don't want to hold things up and carrying out the check too soon defeats the point. If you feel you need an inspection, relations with your vendor probably aren't that great, so it isn't just a matter of you popping round when their removal van is on the doorstep.

Talk it through with your solicitor and the estate agent, but it is worth bothering with, partly because what is left behind can cause as much hassle as what is taken away. If your vendor leaves behind an old fridge, a manky sofa and a clapped-out car (not unknown), you can't simply put them out on the street. However unfair, it's down to you to dispose of them responsibly. (We're tempted to suggest you put them on the front lawn of your vendor's new house, but this might be more trouble than it's worth and entirely goes against our 'be nice to your vendor' policy.)

If you have stuck with us this far it won't surprise you to learn that a successful move is all about preparation.

OUR SUCCESSFUL MOVE STRATEGY

Change of address

The Royal Mail provides a very useful post-forwarding service; you can get a form from your local post office. There is a charge for this, and to a certain extent it is just putting off the evil day; at some point you will have to notify all sorts of people about your change of address.

Among them are your:

- Bank

- Building society. Just because they are lending you the money to buy this new home don't assume that the right hand knows what the left is doing.

- Pension provider

- Other financial service providers. Have you any shares, premium bonds, ISAs, etc?

- Credit and store card companies

- Mobile phone company

- TV cable or satellite company

- Internet service provider

Depending on how far you are moving, you may need to find a whole host of new local services, from GPs to garage mechanics to mole catchers.

UTILITIES

Fortunately, as millions of us move house every year, the utility companies – gas, electricity, water, etc. – have departments that deal with billing alterations and, as a rule, they are efficient and helpful. Telephone companies seem to be less efficient and it never fails to amaze us how expensive and difficult it can be to have new lines installed, sockets moved, and so forth. And make sure you have decent mobile reception at your new home. We travel all over the country, and although most mobile networks claim very high levels of national coverage, there are some patchy bits; if your mobile doesn't work in the area you are moving to, don't assume this is the case for all networks. In the long term you may want to consider changing mobile phone companies.

Are you moving to a new health authority?

If so, inform your current surgery and ask them to send your records to your new surgery. This is something that nobody ever thinks about until they become ill, which is the one time you don't want to be fussing with paperwork. If there is more than one surgery in the area, ask your vendor/estate agent/a friend living locally to recommend a doctor.

Your car is moving house too

You will have to inform your insurance company of your new address and have your driving licence and car registration documents altered. This is particularly important if you are moving to an urban area with a residents' parking permit scheme. Many local authorities will not provide you with a permit until you have the correct address on your documents. There are a mass of costs involved in moving house and you don't want parking tickets to be one of them.

On the subject of parking, don't forget, if you are moving to an urban area where parking is an issue, you will have to have the parking 'suspended' in order for your removal van/lorry to park outside your house. Some firms carry out this chore as part of their service but do remember to discuss it with them well in advance. Many parking authorities require up to a week's notice in order to have the parking suspended. It's not only townies who have such hassles; if you are moving to a rural area where the roads are small and winding, or your new home has a narrow driveway or gate, be sure to inform your removal company and provide them with any relevant measurements. They will be far from happy and may even charge you extra if they have to carry your furniture an extra two hundred yards because their lorry got stuck at the bottom of your drive.

"When my parents moved into their new house, the vendor provided a helpful and comprehensive list of local businesses and services (e.g. newsagent, takeaway restaurants, plumber). It has been frequently photo-copied and scribbled on, but is still pinned up in the kitchen. Many vendors kindly take the trouble to do this, but just to be on the safe side, type out a list of all the people whose numbers you might need and send it to your vendor. All they have to do is fill in the numbers and return it to you or their estate agent."

HUMPING

When you move into your first home, you probably have barely a carload of possessions but, bit by bit, it builds up. By the time you've got to your third or fourth move it involves a pantechnicon and an army of removal men. If you can move your stuff with a hired van and a couple of mates then you'll definitely save yourself some money, but get packing early – trained removal men can judge how large a vehicle they will need, how many boxes are required and how long the move will take just by looking around a house, but to the untrained eye it's less obvious. You may be very surprised by just how much stuff you have and what a major task it is moving it all from A to B. If you intend to employ a removal firm there are a range of levels of service from 'man with a van' to firms whose service is so comprehensive that you can go away on holiday for a week and come back to find that your possessions have been packed, moved, unpacked and put away in your new home.

Ask around for recommendations and get at least three quotes from different firms. It is usually cheaper if you pack yourself, and most companies are happy to drop round some boxes a couple of weeks before the big day. Get packing early. Doing it yourself may mean that you are not insured for breakages inside the boxes, although you should still be covered for damage to furniture if a box is dropped or something is lost. Make sure you discuss this with the removal firm. In addition to the cost saving there are two other major advantages to packing yourself. You have the opportunity to declutter and you can also adopt the 'bingo system' (see over the page).

DECLUTTER

Throw things out! Most of us pay good money to shift stuff that we then throw away when we arrive at the other end. In the chaos of a move, when you have so much to do, making a pile of things to go to your local charity shop or hostel or even simply to be recycled can seem one task too many. And clearly the removal men will not chuck anything away – it's more than their lives are worth. But if you start early you have time to be clear-headed and ruthless. If you have children, ask them to pick out the toys they want to take to their new home, rather than just packing the lot (two stepsons and two sons, I know they won't want to do this but worth a try!). If you discover clothes you haven't worn for years, they will probably look much better on someone else. Kitchen gadgets covered in dust at the back of the cupboard must not join you on your journey. If you haven't used them in this house you won't be overcome by an attack of the Delias in the new place. Freegle and Freecycle are great places to find your unwanted things a new home.

TEA AND SYMPATHY

Unsurprisingly, removal men need constant refuelling. Large amounts of tea, coffee and biscuits, or in the summer cold drinks, are essential, and where possible, sandwiches. We're not suggesting a four-course meal magically provided from the chaos of your new kitchen, but failure to provide suitably adequate refreshments can and does result in a go-slow and you could find that, however clearly you mark all of your boxes, the contents of the kitchen end up in the bedroom. To avoid this unhappy scenario start as you mean to go on: offer them a drink as soon as they arrive. It will be immediately clear that you are the right kind of client, and as a result your removal men will go that extra mile. We've said it before, but moving is hard. You need to get everyone on your side.

BINGO

Whether you're undertaking a DIY move or hiring the grandest removal firm in the land, the following is an excellent method for speeding things up and guaranteeing that the correct boxes and pieces of furniture go to the correct rooms. There is nothing more frustrating than paying out a fortune to a removal firm only to spend the next few weeks carting boxes from room to room yourself, particularly as once opened they are much harder to lift. Coming across five saucepans and the toaster in the spare room doesn't seem funny at 1 a.m. when you are desperately searching for the towels.

THE BINGO SYSTEM

- Make a list of every room in your new home, including the cellar, garage, bathroom, etc.

- Give each room a number. If you're moving to a property similar to your present one, give each room in your current home the corresponding number, so, if the new kitchen is 'Room 3' then your current kitchen should be 'Room 3'.

- Buy some thick black marker pens and as you pack each box mark it, top and sides, with the number of the room that it's heading for. A brief description of the contents is also a great help.

- Make sure everyone in your family knows the number of their new room.

- Also buy a large number of plain stickers and tie-on labels; these are to tag all furniture, pictures, appliances, etc., with their correct number. The reason for this is that apart from the obvious exception of bathrooms and kitchens, when a house is empty it is not clear which room is which. In your mind it may be obvious but without any furniture to indicate a room's purpose in life how is a removal man supposed to know the difference between Mum's room, Sofie's room and the guest room? A removal man's objective is to get the contents of the van into the house as speedily as possible. Even the most conscientious worker is not going to spend long fussing about which room an item (possibly quite heavy) belongs in unless it is clearly marked.

- When you get to the new property, before anyone else sets foot inside, fix to the door and at least two walls of each room large A4 sheets of paper with the number of that room writ large.

This may seem a bit of a bother but we guarantee it will make a huge difference to the speed and efficiency of your move, and you will not be permanently pursued by removal men asking, 'Where's this one going?'

BABY SUITCASE

When expecting a baby, most people have a suitcase packed with essentials ready by the door for weeks before the baby is due, just in case they have to make a dash to the hospital with no time to pack.

When moving house it is a very good idea to have a similar suitcase. The contents may be slightly different but the principle is the same. This and one special packing box come with you in the car and never go near the removal van. You have everything that you need for two days of unpacking, shifting, cleaning and living.

Something will inevitably crop up which we've forgotten to mention, but this strategy does work. We've used it ourselves and anything that makes your move easier is worth a try.

CONTENTS

- change of clothes

- washbag

- towels and one set of sheets, plus duvets and pillows

- any important keys

- passport and driving licence; consider leaving any valuables with friends or family until after the move

- loo roll

- light bulbs

- vacuum cleaner and cleaning paraphernalia

- screwdriver

- sharp knife

- picture-hanging tools

- kettle

- industrial quantities of tea, coffee, milk and sugar, mugs
  – enough for you and the removal men

- two or three plates, bowls, cutlery, one saucepan and/
  or frying pan

- list of important telephone numbers

- torch, candles and matches

- electric heater (winter only)

- mobile/landline telephone and phone charger

- champagne and glasses

10

LIVING THE DREAM

You may well think our job is done. With any luck we've helped you find your new home, hold on to it and move in. We should leave you in peace and stop bossing you about. But that would be a disgraceful dereliction of duty!

Once you have purchased a property, you have to look after it. You've made the biggest investment of your life but it won't be a good investment unless you keep a very close eye on it. It's not like savings – you can't just hand over the money and leave it at that. Your property will always need maintaining, even if you've bought a new-build property.

"The other day I was at my friend Caroline's house and I noticed a small crack in her marble mantelpiece. I had a good look and it was clear that the mantelpiece was coming away from the wall. Had someone leaned hard on it, it could have fallen apart and broken their foot,

or worse. Caroline immediately called a fireplace specialist and they came to take it away. The total cost of removal, repair and reinstallation will be £500. As Caroline said, 'If it's not one thing it's another. Is there no end to it?'"

Here's a list that will get you started on the maintenance habit.

1. Keep your windows clean, particularly if you have wooden window frames, as it's the best way to prevent rot. Hopefully your vendor had a window cleaner and has given you their number. If not, check in the window of the local shop, news-agent or post office, or, failing that, ask the neighbours.

2. Set up a service agreement for the boiler. Nearly all gas suppliers run these schemes and regular services can prolong the life of your boiler and literally save your life.

3. Please, please, please make sure you install numerous smoke alarms and carbon monoxide monitors.

4. Periodically check the attic, basement and any nooks and crannies of your property that you do not use frequently. This is where the rot starts, in more ways than one.

5. Regularly check around the outside of your house, looking for broken guttering or loose tiles. This is particularly impor-tant in winter, when strong winds can dislodge tiles and then you notice water marks appearing on your bedroom ceiling, and in autumn, when fallen leaves can block your gutters,

causing water to pour down the outside walls of your house and encourage damp.

6. Insurance – make sure you have adequate buildings and contents insurance.

7. Make a will – you now have a major asset to bequeath to the cats' home.

8. Set up direct debit payments for the utility bills, council tax and TV licence.

> **PHIL'S TOP TIP**
>
> **If you aren't entirely sure how good you'll be at keeping things up to scratch, then don't replace the carpets until you come to sell the property. That way you won't be living in fear of ruining the new carpet, which would be a real waste of money. And nothing sells a property like good-looking floors.**

We don't want the thought of the horrors that could befall your new home to keep you awake at night. It's just that, having worked so hard to find and secure this property, you may feel you deserve a rest, which is true, but why not make it a working holiday?

You may be intending to stay put for a long time, in which case resale value may not be at the forefront of your mind, but you never know what course life is going to take. Just think, if you were pecked to death by an emu, it would be disappointing if your loved ones, or the cats' home, did not receive as much as they could have simply because you had failed to maintain your property adequately.

We had a client who bought a very nice two-bedroom maisonette in west London. We advised him when he bought it that, as it was in an up-and-coming area, he should view it as a medium-term investment. We also made it clear from the outset that we thought the purchase price a little steep, and as the price of the flat reflected its decor it was important to keep it in mint condition. The vendors were a young couple who had decorated it simply but maximized the light and done everything to make the flat look its best, so it had to be in a similar state when he came to sell if it was going to realize its potential. Less than two years later the client contacted us and he was far from happy. He had decided to sell the flat and had contacted the agent he had bought it from, who came round and valued it. Much to our client's horror, despite a steeply rising market the property had been valued at not much more than he had paid for it, which meant that after stamp duty, agent's fees, etc. he would lose money. We were mystified, and not a little horrified as well, as we pride ourselves on the return our clients get on their investments. We gave the agent a ring and asked what was going on. We knew him well and he didn't pull any punches. 'To be honest,' he replied, 'I was hard pushed to get the valuation as high as I did. That flat is in a right state. He's painted his bedroom dark red. And he's turned the sitting room into a third bedroom, which means the only reception room is the dining area off the kitchen, so the ratio of reception space to bedroom space is completely wrong. The place looks like student digs!' So if you don't think you can keep your flat looking like a new pin, don't buy one that looks like a new pin.

Our book will never be complete because every day we have new property-buying experiences which we want to fill you in on. But what is written here should guide you through 99 per cent of purchasing dilemmas. This cannot be a property Bible, but we hope you have gained knowledge and insight from the gospel of house-buying as preached according to Phil and Kirstie. If it all seems a bit too much like hard work – it is. Did we forget to warn you of that at the beginning? All dreams take effort, so thank your lucky stars that all you want is to buy your own home and not to climb Mount Everest. Keep that train on the track – you're the driver, so make sure everybody knows it – and every time you end up taking a detour and want to thump an agent, don't.

ACKNOWLEDGEMENTS

Phil and I owe huge thanks to my sister, Sofie Allsopp, who took on the task of updating this book with me and to all the directors, producers and house hunters with whom we've learned so much.

KIRSTIE SAYS

"I would like to thank my mum, Fiona Hindlip, who knew more about property than anyone and who helped so much with this book; Georgia, who rebooted at a key stage; and the girls, who are essential."

INDEX

D
damp 59, 131
decluttering 123–4
décor, dated 60
decorating costs 4
deeds 92
deposits, cash 2
details, property 49–50, 83,
    104
district surveyor's certificate
    84
doors 62

E
early housing 27–8
Edwardian 28, 29
electricity 4, 120
*The Elements of Style – An
    Encyclopedia of Domestic
    Architectural Detail* 26
estate agents 43–50, 98–9
    details 49–50, 83, 104
    exchanging contracts
        92–3
    feedback 57–8
    forming relationships
        with xi-xii, 8, 46–9,
        53
    gazumping 74–5

house-hunting business
    cards 5, 44–6
in-house financial
    advisers 68–9
making offers 65–77
memorandum of sale
    78–9
relationship with
    solicitors 96
sealed bids 72–3
surveys 80–3, 102
timetables of sale 87
valuations 36–7
viewings 51–63
exchanging contracts 91–3,
    98–9
same day completion
    105–7, 115

F
family homes 39
finance 1–21
    budgets 1–21
    cash deposits 2
    cost of moving 2, 4
    high-risk borrowers
        16–17
    mortgages 1–3, 5–18
first-time buyers 17–19, 60